MW00776094

Landscape as Sacred Space

God Bless You.

Steve

Landscape as Sacred Space
Metaphors for the Spiritual Journey

Steven Lewis

Cascade Books
A division of Wipf & Stock Publishers
199 West 8th Avenue, Suite 3 • Eugene OR 97401

Landscape as Sacred Space
Metaphors for the Spiritual Journey

Cascade Books
A Division of Wipf and Stock Publishers
199 West 8th Avenue, Suite 3
Eugene, Oregon 97401

ISBN: 1-59752-211-2

Printed in the United States

Contents

Preface

Life is a journey born not of restlessness, but out of the human search for meaning, purpose, identity, and belonging. Spirituality and religion are means to facilitate this journey. More people are looking for fresh ways to embrace their faith and new avenues to explore it. They are searching for better ways to understand, more clearly articulate, and fully develop their spiritual journey, both inside and outside of religious organizations. This search is both complicated and assisted by an increased interest in spirituality, albeit eclectic, that our culture is experiencing in postmodernity. The intention behind this book is to address spiritual searching by utilizing landscape metaphors as invitations for pilgrims to examine the various aspects of their journey as they travel through both the familiar and the mysterious. Three landscapes are particularly dominant on our journey: mountains, deserts, and valleys. These images serve as landmarks to guide our sojourn through this book. I offer this book as an invitation for seekers and saints, all who are willing to reflect honestly on their journey with God through the labyrinth of religion and the wilderness of doubts. It acknowledges mountaintop dwellers, whose desire to remain on spiritual summits often can be blinding to the priceless treasures discovered in spiritual deserts and valleys. It offers assurance and hope for those wandering in spiritual deserts, attempting to understand their feelings of loss and abandonment. This book encourages valley dwellers to discover the sacred in the ordinary as we learn to rest with God. At the heart of this project lies an invitation to a journey with God through the sacred landscapes of our lives to places where we live intentionally in the presence of God.

While the principles of this book address the human spiritual journey, its specific purpose is to speak to Christians, or perhaps those who once considered themselves Christian, about re-imaging their journey with God, using landscape metaphors as common vocabulary and imagery to articulate their faith. Landscape metaphors invite new discussions about our spiritual journeys and allow us to rethink our approaches to Christian spirituality and theology. By utilizing landscape metaphors as common ground for conversation, we can speak to the various dynamics so often associated with our journey with God. We can begin to comprehend why so many struggle with "spiritual depression" and search for a healthy spirituality. This invitation to journey through the various landscapes of life is intended to increase our awareness of God's presence, provide safe spaces for pilgrims to explore their relationship with God in new ways, and grant permission for struggles with God and ourselves. At the same time, it suggests refreshing metaphors that invite exploration and discovery on the journey.

Spiritual mountains, deserts, and valleys are dominant landscapes on our journey through life. Many people have experienced the joy of a mountaintop spiritual experience, the pain of spiritual deserts, or perhaps the dreariness too often associated with spiritual valleys. We have a tendency, however, to highlight spiritual mountaintops, while avoiding spiritual deserts and ignoring spiritual valleys. This leaves many Christians ill-equipped either to deal with crises or to integrate God into ordinary life. It is important to explore spiritual mountains, deserts, and valleys with equal attention and energy. Each landscape offers rich lessons that, when combined together, lead us toward a maturing faith and into a deeper relationship with God.

Landscape metaphors for the Christian spiritual journey are the focus of chapter one. It highlights the potential of landscape metaphors to provide space, permission, and language to journey deeper with God. "Mountaintop Spirituality" will be the first landscape we explore in detail. This very popular and dominant perspective among Christians has much to offer and celebrate; however, it also has led to unrealistic expectations and inadequate understandings of Christianity. Because of the dominant role of mountaintop spirituality among Christians, two chapters address the impact of mountain terrains on the Christian journey. Chapter two explores the highlights of mountaintop spirituality, focusing on issues of familiarity, intimacy, and trust. Chapter three unpacks the negative implications of mountaintop spirituality in relation to spiritual deserts and valleys. Other important spiritual terrains can be ignored when spiritual mountains become one's sole focus. Chapter four explores the value of "Desert Spirituality," with its wide range of emotions, to our faith journey. Spiritual deserts are vital, yet difficult landscapes for Christian pilgrimages to navigate. The desert is paradoxical by nature, calling us to release and embrace, providing a clarity that is accompanied by a "holy ambiguity." Chapter five turns to the less recognized, yet critical landscape of spiritual "Valleys." Spiritual valleys are the dominant terrain of our lives; yet they are the easiest to ignore. Valleys are the landscape where we work, play, rest, and set up daily life. Together, these three landscapes provide access to something that is already in our hearts and minds, the presence of God. The terrains simply invite us to reflect on our journeys with God through the various experiences of our lives. The landscapes provide environments that open our imaginations to new understandings of God and ourselves. Finally, I draw together the various lessons from the spiritual landscapes and explore how they empower us to live mindfully in the presence of God as everyday mystics with a deeply rooted social consciousness as we live out the ministry of Jesus in the world.

Navigating through the current, culturally accepted, spiritual landscapes is a difficult and complicated task. In recent years, numerous books have been written about spirituality from a variety of perspectives, addressing both individual and community spirituality. It is not necessary to rehearse the details of those works in this project. There is general agreement that we live in a period of increased spiritual hunger that has its roots in the rise of postmodernity in the latter part of the twentieth century. Spiritual themes permeate movies, advertisements, talk shows, and casual conversations. This renewed interest in spirituality, like those of the past, is passionately connected to humanity's search for meaning, purpose, identity, and belonging. Increased interest in spirituality, from the rise of the "New Age" movements to a flood of pilgrims entering monastic retreat centers, to the advent of psychic hotlines, all serve as testimonies to the spiritual awakening that has taken hold in our era. A hunger to know more fully the divine presence, to encounter the Spirit of God and embrace grace, stand in direct relationship with a spirituality that is more eclectic than ever. This eclectic spiritual environment has stimulated many Christians to reconsider the importance of their own faith journey and to evaluate the adequacy both of their spirituality and of their religious communities.

Limitations

While the principles of this project may be applied in numerous settings, I must admit its deep connections to a North American Christian context. Mountaintop spirituality is a dominant paradigm among a large number of North American Christians. It is so intertwined within the Christian consciousness that it goes virtually unnoticed. While mountaintop spirituality is not exclusive to North America, it blends with political and social ideologies that seamlessly lead us to conclude that we are called and destined to "be on top." In contrast, liberation theologies often form and are articulated in spiritual deserts, emerging out of struggle; and they draw strength and identity from engaging in that struggle. It would be insulting to suggest mountaintop paradigms are dominant spiritual forms in liberation theologies.

The three landscapes developed in this book reflect what I believe are the dominant popular Christian understandings. I utilize desert images to denote harsh, difficult terrain through which we travel on our spiritual sojourns. Spiritual desert imagery, however, fits into a larger metaphor of wilderness experiences. Wilderness metaphors may be applied to a variety of landscapes. St. Brendan the Navigator utilized the ocean as a wilderness metaphor. He spoke of "a desert in the ocean," something that perhaps only makes sense when understood from his Celtic perspective.[1] The valley also can stimulate wilderness imagery with its swamps and bogs. Mountains can represent lush green resting places as well as harsh rocky steep terrains that are difficult to traverse. Mountain imagery can contrast the fertile images of Mt. Carmel and Mt. Tabor with the harsh rocky slopes of Mt. Sinai.[2] Wilderness metaphors may vary; however, the experiences and values of the wilderness sojourn are similar. I have chosen to utilize desert imagery due to its common appeal to our imaginations. I have also chosen to highlight mountains as lush, restful environments due to the popular understanding of mountaintop spirituality.

An additional limitation centers in my selection of landscapes. Numerous conversations over the last few years have focused on this limitation. Many have asked, "Why only three landscapes: mountains, deserts, and valleys?" Largely because these three terrains are familiar and dominant landscapes in our lives. Most of us have experienced mountaintop encounters and dry spiritual deserts while struggling to accept and draw comfort from the ordinary of the valley. Oceans, rivers, lakes, and seas have often been offered as additional landscapes to explore. Perhaps future work can develop these landscapes as spiritual metaphors for our journey.

Acknowledgments

There are many people I wish to thank for their support of this project. Belden Lane first introduced me to the fascinating ideas of landscapes as sacred places while I was a doctoral student at Saint Louis University. I am forever grateful for his gift to my imagination. I hope my work honors the principles Belden introduced to me fifteen years ago.

I am grateful for the critiques and suggestions from my colleagues in the Religion department at Warner Pacific College. I am particularly thankful for Stephen Carver's supportive friendship and encouragement as I worked on this project. Gloria Law, Jay Barber, Lou Foltz, Bryan Williams, and so many others at Warner Pacific College were vital to this project. Thank you, friends.

Edsel White and the staff at the First United Methodist Church in Vancouver, Washington, were thoughtful enough to invite me to serve as Theologian in Residence, allowing me to write the majority of the manuscript while on a study leave from the academy. They gave so much more to me than I was able to return to them. This project would have never been finished without their support.

I would like to thank especially the numerous students who endured my Spiritual Formation classes over the past ten years. They were the original impetus for this project. This book emerged from the spiritual struggles of students whose spiritual journeys too often resembled roller coasters, with dramatic ups and downs void of deeper reflection and hope. Landscape metaphors facilitated the conversations toward healthy and more balanced spirituality.

My friend and spiritual director, Bill Zuelke, provided valuable insights into the manuscript. Our conversations are woven into the fabric of the book. His wisdom and guidance enriched this project. Marjo Mitsutomi, my good friend and colleague, was vital in the early stages of this book. Her linguistic skills and spiritual insights opened my imagination to new possibilities. I wish to thank my family. My parents, Sadie and Art, instilled a determination within me to dream dreams and work to make them come true. My father taught me to explore life and knowledge as a young child, and my mother instilled the thought that I could do anything I put my mind to. They gifted me with a simple desire to help other people and a realization that nothing is worth having if one cannot share it. My father's recent Christian commitment was continually in my mind as the book developed, especially as I explored the sections on mountaintop spirituality, which is often the entering place for the spiritual journey.

Finally, I offer my greatest thanks to my wife Renee and my children Lindsey and Grant, who have been willing to allow some of their stories to be told in the pages of this book. They have given me more happiness than any one person could ever wish for. God blessed me with a wonderful wife and friend whom I have known since I was sixteen years old. We have traveled through the various spiritual landscapes together as pilgrims on a sacred journey. The birth of Lindsey and Grant will forever remain two of the greatest mountaintop experiences in my life. They were also the first to teach me to see the sacred in the ordinary. Their love and patience have permanently changed my life.

I will forever be a student of the mysteries of God, passionately searching for ways to invite people on a journey with God to the deepest places of life.

Steven Lewis
Ordinary Time 2004

Endnotes

1. See David Adam, *A Desert in the Ocean: The Spiritual Journey according to St. Brendan the Navigator* (New York: Paulist, 2000).
2. Belden Lane, *The Solace of Fierce Landscapes* (New York: Oxford Univ. Press, 1998), does a wonderful job of developing the contrast between Mt. Tabor and Mt. Sinai. See chapter five in particular (124–40).

1

Landscape Metaphors

Navigating the Spiritual Journey

Landscape metaphors provide a common language and familiar imagery through which to articulate and critique the Christian spiritual journey. Most people can imagine what a mountaintop spiritual experience is like, with its warm fuzzy feelings and renewed spiritual energy. The pure excitement of a close encounter with God stirs our imaginations and awakens us to the reality of God's presence. On the other end of the emotional spectrum, most people also know the loneliness and fear of a spiritual desert. The spiritual deserts are often filled with confusion, fear, and empty spaces, which we interpret as divine abandonment. In addition, there is another, less recognized landscape—the valley, or the ordinary. By its very nature, the ordinary goes unnoticed. The valley is the place where we dwell, grow, work, and play. It is our spiritual home, to which we return after our sojourns into the spiritual deserts or our visits to the mountaintops.

A growing number of Christians are searching for safe spaces to wrestle with their faith, permission to ask hard questions, and fresh language that invites discovery of God in deeper ways. Landscape metaphors provide a common language and space to explore one's journey with God. Metaphors invite and, on a certain level, even grant us permission to struggle in spiritual deserts, rejoice in the mountaintop experiences, and embrace valleys as spiritual places where the ordinary becomes sacred. Utilizing landscape metaphors as a means to explore common spiritual experiences can stimulate the exploration and discovery that many Christians are seeking in their relationships with God.

Safe Space

Safe space is vital to spiritual development. One must have an environment that enables exploration and encourages expression while fostering trust and authenticity. Safe spaces allow us to be honest and vulnerable as we explore who we really are. The church is not always a safe space to rehearse deep spiritual questions. It is not always receptive to challenging questions that relate to beliefs, structure, and relevance. Asking deep theological questions can lead to conflict with fellow Christians and church authorities. Brian McLaren lamented: "You cannot talk about this sort of thing [deeper questions of our faith] with just anybody. People worry about you. They think you have changed sides, turning traitor."[1] Asking faith questions can be very difficult and stressful. I have witnessed the pain that many college students experience as they begin the process of owning their faith. They desire support and dialogue with their faith community, close friends, and family; but all too often many receive reprimands for raising faith questions about tradition, doctrines, or practices. Safe spaces are needed for pilgrims who struggle with their faith and wrestle with theological, political, and social issues as they journey with God. Loving and supportive environments are needed to allow pilgrims to discover and explore their journey with God while placing their discoveries in the context of their faith community.

Permission

In addition to safe spaces, pilgrims need permission to encounter God honestly in the deeper parts of the soul, going beyond the superficial religiosity that too often has come to characterize segments of Christianity. It sounds overly simplistic to suggest that people need or desire permission to think and question; but in matters of faith, Christians are often afraid to raise serious queries about their faith experiences. Faith questions can lead to confusion, struggle, isolation, and spiritual deserts. However, raising questions is a way of learning, and a consequence of growth and development, much like that of children. Still, raising faith questions can pose certain challenges to dominant paradigms. If Christians cannot honestly raise questions of their faith, flowing from their journeys with God, then we have stifled spiritual exploration, the religious imagination, and an opportunity for God to speak afresh into the lives of numerous Christians. Safe spaces and permission work together to create an environment that enables and invites faith exploration and ownership.

Some faith communities provide environments of exploration, but lack the willingness or courage to allow God to speak freely to pilgrims on a spiritual journey. Communities can develop a myopic focus that directs spiritual exploration solely toward social issues or "Me and Jesus" encounters. In so doing, they impede pilgrims' quest for rich, fulfilling, and balanced spirituality.

Language

Along with safe space and permission, there is a need for fresh language— symbols and metaphors to aid in the expression and articulation of the Christian faith journey. In some cases, what may be needed is the renewal and reclaiming of old symbols or metaphors, which can be given new life in a postmodern context. Religious language has the potential to limit our spiritual quest and divide people. It also has the capability to invite exploration and discovery, providing access to experiences and allowing individuals and communities to articulate encounters with God in fresh and creative ways. "A good metaphor moves us to see our ordinary world in an extraordinary way."[2] Landscape metaphors represent older symbols that can be reclaimed in our current environment. Mountain, desert, and valley metaphors can provide a common language that allows us to see the ordinary in extraordinary ways. These metaphors can give access to our experiences with God and a greater means to articulate and critique our faith journeys. The purpose for a common language is not to restrict spiritual expressions, but simply to serve as a starting place for those who need assistance articulating their faith experiences. Utilizing landscape metaphors does not attempt to create new containers to limit spiritual experiences within the context of any religious group. Although language has the potential to contain and limit experiences, replacing the mysterious with the explainable, it can also aid in the exploration and discovery of God in deeper and more meaningful ways. Landscape metaphors provide a common language, a starting place that invites us on a journey of transformation and enables conversation without confining spiritual experiences to old paradigms. We must always use religious language carefully. Our attempts to describe spiritual experiences often end up being limiting or confining and, as a result, make it harder to understand. Landscapes are vessels, expansive metaphors, meeting places to stimulate our imaginations and spiritual conversations.

Exploring Spiritual Landscapes

Mountains, valleys, and deserts are common physical and spiritual terrains of humanity; however, navigating these spiritual terrains is neither easy nor natural for most of us. While these landscapes generate a familiarity that resonates with our spiritual journey and life experiences on one level, they also present us with feelings of confusion, fear, frustration, and loss. One might be surprised, however, to realize how much these landscape metaphors are played out in the life of the church. For centuries, the Church calendar has aided individuals and communities in their explorations of these various landscapes experiences. The liturgical calendar is one way that Christians consciously interact and move through the various spiritual landscapes. The three major spiritual landscapes of life are highlighted by the Church calendar. Advent invites us on the journey up the mountain to the celebration of Christmas. We anticipate the arrival at the peak and receive clarity as we approach the summit of the mountain with the Christmas celebration. Epiphany represents the slow journey down the mountain back into the valley, into the ordinary. After eight weeks of ordinary time, dwelling in the valley, we enter the desert sojourn of Lent that climaxes in Passion Week with the crucifixion. Easter brings

4

us to another mountaintop experience, which continues to Pentecost. Finally, we return to the valley for a long season of ordinary time. The liturgical calendar is another way to sensitize us to the active presence of God, reminding us that God is present in all of the landscapes and seasons of life. It highlights and values each of the landscapes, allowing us to glean the rich lessons they offer. The liturgical calendar offers one means to navigate these landscapes, providing a healthy rhythm that invites us to journey through the spiritual terrains and experience the gamut of human emotions while reinforcing the presence of God in all of our experiences. The Church calendar simply highlights the natural rhythm of our lives: the ups, the downs, and the normal.

Mountaintop Spirituality

Mountaintop spirituality is both a conscious and unconscious standard from which numerous Christians from multiple denominations and movements function. A mountaintop mentality, however, is not limited to spiritual arenas. It parallels other aspects of American culture. Corporate models and Christian mountaintop mentality affirm many of the same elements of life. Both construct strategies to remain at the top and often consult with others about how they too can reside at the summit. They instill confidence and celebrate success. Corporate America has influenced church growth programs, architectural designs of church buildings, and leadership structures. Mountaintop spirituality can represent a spiritual dominance that does not equally empower, encourage, and enable all pilgrims on their journeys with God. Instead, it fosters competitiveness and ignorance. Therefore, it is vital that this form of spirituality be honestly explored and analyzed. Mountaintop spirituality is a very popular form that places a great amount of focus on heightened spiritual experiences. This form of mountaintop spirituality generally views mountains as lush, green, inviting, and playful places. It concentrates on spiritual euphoria and an intense spiritual energy that often accompanies mountain encounters. It highlights the best parts of the Christian experience and builds a spirituality around them. Mountaintop spirituality has much to offer pilgrims; in fact, mountaintop experiences are important to spiritual formation. Valuable lessons come from our mountaintop encounters—lessons of familiarity, intimacy, and trust. The most important component is our ability to apply those lessons to the various spiritual landscapes that we encounter on our journey with God. Mountaintop experiences provide references for our understanding of God and stimulate a desire to walk continually with God; however, they can also lead to an unbalanced spirituality.

While there are many strengths of mountaintop spirituality, a number of issues also arise from this perspective. First, it tends to limit spiritual exploration to lush mountaintops, while ignoring wilderness mountain imageries, which is also rooted in biblical and historical narratives. A holistic mountain spirituality is paradoxical in nature, holding in tension mountains as inviting resting places along with mountains as harsh wildernesses. The popular form of mountain spirituality, however, is often unbalanced and encourages a reluctance to move beyond the familiarity and warmth of spiritual mountains into the mysterious deserts, valleys, or alternative concepts of mountains, which also offer important lessons for our journey with God. Christian maturity and divine intimacy are often generated through authentic struggles with our faith as we journey through the various landscapes of our lives. Attempts to avoid spiritual deserts and valleys only exacerbate an unbalanced spirituality.

There is a delicate balance between affirming mountaintop spirituality and realizing that mountaintops represent only one type of spiritual landscape among many. Some Christians are able to navigate their way through life, moving from one mountaintop to another while spending very little time in other terrains. Deserts and valleys serve only as brief transitional landscapes that connect mountaintops. These Christians virtually ignore the value of spiritual deserts and valleys and focus almost exclusively on ascending the mountain and staying at the top as long as possible. Growing numbers of Christians are becoming disillusioned and struggle with their Christianity because they cannot maintain a spirituality clothed in emotional highs and warm fuzzy experiences. They struggle to understand and embrace the other spiritual landscapes that they encounter. Doubt, fear, loneliness, and even anger accompany them on their journey and serve only to further complicate the situation. At times, mountaintop spirituality can seem out of touch with real life struggles, causing too many Christians to avoid and ignore a holistic understanding of the journey with God. However, the historic writings of the "Desert Fathers and Mothers" revealed priceless lessons how one could mindfully dwell with

God, release the baggage of life, embrace God's grace, receive a clarity of vision unique to the desert, and rest in holy ambiguity.

Desert Spirituality

The second major landscape explored in this book is the spiritual desert. Spiritual deserts have a haunting familiarity for most of us, because we have experienced the desert firsthand. The desert requires a transparency, vulnerability, honesty, and openness that enable a deeper experience with God. Deserts identify those things that would distract us or stand in the way of a more intimate relationship with God. However, the path to intimacy is through honest reflection, which can lead to struggle. The spiritual desert is often a place of struggle, exploration, and discovery of God and of ourselves. It can be a very sacred place to encounter God and ourselves, or it can be a place where we are lost in our own selfishness and anger.

Spiritual deserts are generally scary places. Everything about them is foreign to us. The harsh environment does not attract us nor resemble anything that we have come to associate with God. A number of intense emotions accompany us on the desert journey, which only adds to the difficulty of the sojourn. Anger, confusion, loss, disorientation, and abandonment are only a sampling of the feelings that we experience in the desert. However, the desert can help us more clearly understand who we are and how we relate to God. The desert facilitates a clarity of vision, a release of baggage, an opportunity to embrace grace, and a willingness to rest in "holy ambiguity." The desert can, if we allow it, be a deeply spiritual place to draw closer to God. Sometimes we just need a little help to re-envision the spiritual desert as a sacred place to walk with God, to identify and release those things in life that are barriers on our walk.

Valley Dwelling

The third terrain explored is the valley. Spiritual valleys are under utilized and under appreciated in the Christian spiritual journey; however, they are the primary terrains of our lives. Valley spirituality equally values and embraces spiritual deserts and mountains as vital parts of a holistic journey with God. Compared to the mountaintop approach, spiritual valleys may appear less glamorous and less intimate with God. However, spiritual valleys foster an incarnational reality, which is a cornerstone of Christian spirituality. Incarnational reality is simply the realization that God is manifested within us, through Christ, enabling us to envision and embrace God as a constant companion on our journey. This heightened awareness of God empowers our capability to be valley dwellers and envision the ordinary as a sacred space. If we embody the reality that God is dwelling within us through the power of the Spirit of God, then we are inclined to see God actively engaged in the ordinary.

Spiritual valleys invite us to dwell mindfully in the presence of God and to re-envision the spiritual journey not as a series of ups and downs, going to and from mountaintops, but as pilgrimages through the various landscapes of life with God as our companion. A valley perspective emphasizes the immanence of God, that is, God's presence in us and in the ordinary things of life. When we embrace the notion that God dwells in us, our entire outlook on life is transformed. Motivated by incarnational reality, valley dwellers desire to be like Jesus, embodying God's presence, spreading God's love, and speaking to injustices that separate us from God and one another.

Like any spiritual approach, valley spirituality has weaknesses. Complacency is perhaps its greatest weakness. The ordinary can easily become the unnoticed, the normal, the regular, and thus we begin to miss God's revelations around us. Driving the kids to soccer games can be just another routine in our day, or it can be an occasion to see God's expressions in children, nature, and others around us. As we become comfortable with life in the valley, we can get distracted and adapt to a routine, numbed to God's presence and caught up in the business of life. It is difficult at times to maintain our awareness and continue to dwell mindfully in God's presence. It takes intentionality and some amount of discipline to dwell mindfully in the presence of God.

As pilgrims on a journey, we often struggle to comprehend God's indwelling in and through us. God empowers us to express love, grace, mercy, and compassion to the world around us. Incarnational reality suggests that God desires to be birthed in us, to be expressed through our imaginations, creativity, and acts of mercy and grace. We are called to be like Christ, who modeled the indwelling presence of God in a way humanity had not seen before or since. Valley spirituality takes seriously the call to be Christ to the world and mindfully dwell in the presence of God in a way that empowers us to see the extraordinary in the simplest things of life.

Living in the Presence: Walking with God through the Landscapes of Life

Metaphorical mountains, deserts, and valleys provide us with diverse, yet equally valuable experiences that enhance our relationship with God. Each of these landscapes grants unique insights into ourselves and our understanding of God. When we bring the valuable insights from each landscape together, we begin to see life anew. We start to understand how we can mindfully live in the presence of God. This type of existence flows from a process of awareness, humility, openness, desire, and intentionality, which allows us to transform the totality of life into sacred spaces. Once our awareness of God's presence is heightened, all of life's landscapes provide us with an opportunity to dwell mindfully with God.

Several historical characters serve as examples of those who learned to live mindfully in the presence of God. Ann Wall, Brother Lawrence, and Celtic Christians are just a few examples. Ann's journey from fear to intimacy on her sojourn with God was through the desert. She learned to be comfortable and rest in God's presence through the various trials of her life. Ann modeled intentionality through adversity. A seventeenth-century lay brother, commonly known as Brother Lawrence, contributed further insight into how we can "Practice the Presence of God." Brother Lawrence provided insight into how we can turn the mundane valley into an act of worship and practice the presence of God in the normal routines of life. He gave testimony to the importance of true desire in one's spiritual life. Finally, Celtic Christian spirituality provides great insight into our search for ways to dwell mindfully in the presence of God. The Celts highlighted the concept of "thin places," that experience of the mountaintop where abilities to perceive God were greatly enhanced. However, they did not make a great distinction between the secular and the sacred but instead invited others to see God in all things of life. By blurring the lines between the secular and the sacred, the Celts advocated a greater awareness of God in all things in life. They were open and receptive to God's movement in the world. Ann, Brother Lawrence, and the Celts provide us with useful aids to explore ways to live mindfully in the presence of God in all of the spiritual landscapes of life.

The contemplative life is not reserved for monastic communities. We too can live out an everyday mysticism while understanding the social implications of our salvation. In our ever increasingly busy lives, it takes intentionality to make spaces for prayer, reflection, reading inspirational texts, and investing in others. Living mindfully in the presence of God is not a heavenly rehearsal for the afterlife. It is a place from which to reach out to others with the love of God.

Spiritual Imagination

The development and nurture of the spiritual imagination is one key element of the journey through life's landscapes. The imagination helps shape and orient our perceptions of life.[3] According to Richard Kearney the "imagination lies at the very heart of our existence. So much so that we would not be human without it."[4] It stimulates our spiritual journey, prayer life, worship, and understanding of God. Without the imagination, the spiritual journey would be dull and fruitless.[5]

Some forms of Christianity engage the imagination more than others. For some, the "smells and bells" of rituals and worship stimulate the imagination, enabling the Spirit of God to move through the mind and heart. Other Christian groups and denominations, however, approach the imagination with great suspicion and reluctance. As a child I was cautioned that the mind can be the playground for the devil. I was a young adult before I realized that the mind was in fact the playground for God. This revelation allowed me to recapture a vital aspect of my spirituality.

The imagination is an avenue toward a rediscovery of our spirituality and a fresh view at God. The origin and power of religion are at the imaginative level both for individuals and faith communities.[6] Unfortunately, as we grow older we tend to lose the power of imagination. As children, we saw things that were not there, talked to invisible people, saw characters in the clouds, employed our imaginations, and transformed swing sets into space ships. For many children, the mind is a playground for God and the imagination a vehicle into an amazing world in which

God is ever present. By the time we reach our young adult years, we begin to ignore our imaginations and rely on our intellect to reveal God's mysteries, which generally leaves us disappointed. We trade our imaginations for realism in a world that tells us to grow up and see the world as it is, not as it can be. As a result, we have forgotten what God looks like and how to live out of the depths of our experiences with God. Accessing our imagination helps us to recall the lessons from our sojourn, to discover, imagine, play, and encounter God at the very essence of our beings. Simply put, we need to recover or at least re-envision a religious imagination.[7] The imagination is vital to our faith journey and must be recovered from the grip of modernity.[8]

Spiritual Maturity

Not only do we need to recover the imagination of our childhood, we need to reclaim natural gifts that enable our spiritual maturity. We spend much of our lives in search of meaning, purpose, identity, and belonging. Reclaiming our "birthright gifts" and our childhood imaginations prepares us for the sojourn through spiritual terrains; however, we must balance the gifts of childhood with the call to spiritual maturity. We are called to a deeper, more fulfilling walk with God that requires serious reflection and contemplation. Nonetheless, we must never lose the desire to approach God as a child—innocent, imaginative, playful, dependent, and in need of guidance. At times, a childlike understanding of God is appropriate, but on other occasions mature reflection is needed to embrace God.

Our journey often requires us to rethink our understandings of and relationship with God. Our perceptions of most things in life develop as we mature; however, our concept of God often does not. Too often, the only difference between a five-year-old and fifty-year-old Sunday school class presentation is the use of pictures in the former. At some point, many of us were given a theological package that contained the guidelines for our religious understanding. Some of these packages were general, lacking specificity; however, other religious packages contained detailed outlines of doctrine that were meant to be internalized and memorized so others could be evangelized. The one thing most of us were not encouraged to do was to raise questions about our theological package. Questions posed a certain danger to a well-defined theological understanding. As a result, many Christians have not reflected on their faith because reflection and questions can be dangerous to established religious practices and thought. The result is a spiritual poverty that exists among numerous Christians, leaving them unable or unwilling to engage God outside of limited mountaintop paradigms. Many remain unaware of their "spiritual poverty" and continue to rehearse spiritual forms that lack significance and meaning. Too many people settle for a spirituality that consists of occasional mountaintop experiences with long periods of spiritual depression and call it normal.

Spiritual struggles, faith crises, spiritual highs, and experiences of discovering the sacred in the ordinary are all essential for our transformation and maturation with God. Our experiences may be difficult, revealing, and draining; but they pave the road to a deeper embodiment of God. In any relationship that we desire to cultivate, including our relationship with God, we must be willing to embrace the celebrations and the struggles of life as equal parts on our journey. Our fear of the uncomfortable leads many of us to desire and remain on spiritual mountaintops while ignoring the equally valuable landscapes of valleys and deserts. This book invites the reader to receive the lessons that each landscape has to teach us and sit with God, who beckons us to become more comfortable with the divine and to dwell mindfully with God through all of life's terrains.

Conclusion

Navigating the spiritual landscapes of our lives often happens on "autopilot." We are not always conscious of the terrains on our journeys. We simply experience the joys and sorrows of life without deeper reflection. Landscape metaphors for the spiritual journey are only one means to promote a more conscious examination of our relationship with God as we go through life. The metaphors are intended to heighten our awareness of the divine and aid us in the application of lessons gained from our experiences with God to life around us.

This book is an invitation to reflect honestly on our journey with God through the spiritual landscapes of life. However, opening ourselves to God's voice may necessitate a re-envisioning of the spiritual journey in a more holistic way that appreciates a variety of spiritual landscapes. Each spiritual terrain presents challenges to our dominant paradigms, and it is difficult to develop a holistic spirituality if we avoid certain topographies while exclusively embracing others. It is natural to desire comfort over discomfort, or familiarity over mystery; however, life does not always afford us the option to avoid adversities. We must learn to see God in suffering as well as joy, in sorrow and celebration, in the ordinary and the extreme. In the process, our spiritual journey may just become more than we ever envisioned, as we begin to realize that we are so much more than we think we are.

God is calling us to embrace adventure, to take risks, to re-envision, to open ourselves to the movement of the Holy Spirit, and to embrace the sacred wherever it may reside. The call to a journey of adventure through spiritual landscapes involves risk and struggle; but where there is no risk, there is no adventure, and where there is no struggle, there is no growth.[9] If we make comfort and money our goals in life, we will measure our lives by how much comfort we have achieved and how much money we have collected. If we make God's will our goal, we will be called to adventure.[10] May this book be a source of clarity for the journey made and a source of hope for the journey to come.

Endnotes

1. Brian McLaren, *A New Kind of Christian: A Tale of Two Friends on a Spiritual Journey* (San Francisco: Jossey-Bass, 2001), xv.
2. Sallie McFague, *Speaking in Parables: A Study in Metaphor and Theology* (Philadelphia: Fortress, 1975), xvi.
3. Sharon Daloz Parks, *Big Questions, Worthy Dreams: Mentoring Young Adults in Their Search for Meaning, Purpose, and Faith* (San Francisco: Jossey-Bass, 2000), 108.
4. Richard Kearney, *Poetics of Imagining: Modern to Post-Modern* (New York: Fordham Univ. Press, 1998), 1.
5. Thomas Merton, *Contemplation in a World of Action* (Notre Dame: Notre Dame Univ. Press, 1998), 357.
6. Andrew Greeley, *The Catholic Imagination* (Berkeley: Univ. of California Press, 2000), 4.
7. Catholic writers like Andrew Greeley and David Tracy have done some wonderful work with faith and imagination. Protestant writers need to develop more research in the area of the Protestant imagination.
8. Kearney, *Poetics of Imagining*.
9. David Adam, *A Desert in the Ocean: The Spiritual Journey According to St. Brendan the Navigator* (New York: Paulist, 2000), 1.
10. Ibid., 29.

2
Mountaintop Spirituality 1
Lessons from the Mountaintops

Of the three landscapes that we will explore in this book, mountaintop terrains are perhaps the most familiar. Consciously or unconsciously, mountaintop spirituality is one of the most popular ways Christians describe their spiritual journeys. While valley and desert metaphors may remain less familiar images for our spiritual sojourn, mountaintop metaphors resonate with believers. Most Christians know what a mountaintop experience is like although they may lack the language to describe it. The popularity of mountaintop spirituality centers around heightened spiritual experiences and the dramatic transformations that often accompany them. These experiences are frequently associated with one's initial conversion, church camp experiences, retreats, or other especially focused spiritual experiences. They become foundational references for what God feels like to us while inspiring our desire to walk with God. The use of mountaintop spirituality as a dominant paradigm of the Christian journey transcends mainline and evangelical denominational identities. It applies to all Christians who interpret their spirituality through a mountaintop lens, to those who continually seek spiritual euphoria and emotional invigoration. While numerous issues arise from this perspective, these heightened sacred encounters are vital parts of our spiritual formation. They serve as reference points for our journey with God and are often the first landscape we acknowledge on our spiritual journey.

The intent of this chapter is to affirm the major strengths of mountaintop spirituality and yet invite the reader to consider carefully some of its inherent weaknesses that may encumber spiritual formation. By exploring both the strengths and weaknesses of mountaintop experiences, I hope to help readers embrace the valuable lessons that mountains have to teach us.

The Value of the Mountaintop

We begin our journey with the mountaintop metaphor because it is a dominant form of Christian spirituality. Mountaintop encounters confirm God's presence and stimulate our determination to walk in the ways of the Lord. These mountaintop experiences, however, vary greatly among individuals and communities.

People experience and process encounters with God differently. The dynamics of our divine relationship evolve as God works within our personalities, temperaments, and imaginations to speak to our hearts and reveal grace in a way that we can understand and receive. Our experiences with God do share commonalities, but mountain encounters resist a one size fits all standard. The commonalities frequently involve an intense awareness of God's presence. For some, this takes the form of peaceful, reflective time with God that does not generate any particular spiritual high, but instills a deep sense of God's presence. The mountain simply facilitates sitting with God, receiving blessings and direction before returning to the valley. As the Old Testament character Moses evolved in his relationship with God, mountaintop encounters became less traumatic and dramatic for him. He learned simply to rest in the presence of God, enter into dialogue about life, and receive assurance before returning to the valley to share some of his experiences with others. This type of mountaintop encounter may seem foreign to some; however, mountaintop moments may simply bring us to a place of rest and reflection. There is no overly dramatic experience, but we are, nonetheless, transformed. For many, however, mountaintop experiences are monumental moments marked by emotional highs, occasions of spiritual euphoria, feelings of intense emotional warmth, with an overwhelming sense of divine presence. Mountain experiences serve as landmarks for the journey, with God reminding us of what divine intimacy is like. Both types of mountaintop encounters have value and teach us similar lessons; however, it seems that the majority of Christians experience mountaintops as dynamic landscapes. I was recently reminded of the excitement and importance of dynamic mountaintop experiences when I visited my father. Dad became a Christian in his mid-sixties. His excitement is contagious. His joy is both evident and overflowing to all of those around him. He sees life through the eyes of a new believer who has just met God and has been transformed. My dad has found a home and comfort in the mountaintop metaphor. He has a passion to serve and know God more. He awakes with prayers that flow from his desire to allow God to lead him through the day, and he falls asleep to prayers of thanksgiving. Scripture is a vital part of his day even though he admits that there is much he does not understand. For him, all of life becomes an opportunity to experience God, whose love is overwhelming. The passion in his heart overcomes him when he attempts to put his divine experiences into words. As we talked about his spiritual journey, we found ourselves resting in those places where words are unspoken, but love is experienced and the presence of God is enveloping. These are moments when "deep speaks to deep, spirit speaks to spirit, and heart speaks to heart."[1] The apostle Paul encouraged the Romans to rest in those places where words did not come. "The Spirit helps us in our weakness; for we do not know how to pray as we ought, but that very Spirit intercedes with sighs too deep for words" (Romans 8:26 NRSV).[2] For now, Dad dwells on a spiritual mountaintop, a comfortable and safe place to begin a journey with God, a place of words and silence.

Mountaintop experiences place us in a holy tension of expression and silence. Caught between two ancient paradoxical traditions, the "kataphatic" and "apophatic" ways, we search for avenues to understand God. The apophatic way suggests that human categories are incapable of conceptualizing God. There are no words, images, or thoughts that can adequately describe God. We are left with silence in recognition of the utter poverty of language.[3] We are left to rest in silence and the movement of the Holy Spirit. In contrast, the kataphatic approach employs the use of images, thoughts, imagination, music, poetry, and more, making generous use of metaphor to understand and describe God. Neither understanding is sufficient; we need a healthy balance of both traditions. Sometimes we need only sit and receive the blessings of God. In those silent moments, God's presence swells up from within and we are moved beyond language. God consumes us and we become more than we thought possible. Somehow, in some way, God is manifested in us in ways that words cannot express. Attempts to put into words that which we have experienced leads to the evaporation of the moment and sometimes the loss of the blessing. On the other hand, there are times when our encounters with God lead to a depth of creativity and expressiveness. Wonderful paintings, musical compositions, poems, and many more creative expressions stand as testimonies of divine-human encounters.

Just like Peter when he saw the transfigured Christ, we are caught in the tension between expression and silence, between fear and a desire to commemorate what we have experienced, between resting in God's blessings and a creative response. We simply know that it has been good to be in God's presence and that we long to stay in the embrace of the moment (Matthew 17:4). Peter wanted to remain on the mountain and build "three dwellings" to signify his experience of the transfigured Christ and mark the site as sacred, but Jesus would not allow it, perhaps because he knew words could not adequately describe the encounter. Music, art, poetry, stories, even architecture have for centuries served as expressions of the divine-human encounter, but not all encounters warrant commemoration. As with Peter, Jesus moves us back down the mountain into the valley where we re-engage the world around us and ponder God's wonders in our hearts, learning to express our experiences in ways that may bless others. An immense temptation arises from the mountaintop to set up camp and stay, but it would be a great error to stay on the mountaintop and attempt to dwell there. The divine call to intimacy can easily be confused with the desire to remain on the mountain. Mountaintops are often the first experience with divine intimacy, making it natural to equate the experience of intimacy with metaphorical mountains. However, when the spiritual euphoria has waned, we are left to wonder why and how our great excitement could have diminished. We tend to ask, "Where has God gone?" rather than realize that God is with us in the ordinary things of life as well as the extraordinary. So, we search for other spiritual experiences that will lead us back to the mountaintop and we begin a cycle that is not always fulfilling or spiritually healthy.

Ultimately, mountaintops provide rest and blessed experiences for us. They are safe environments to rest with God, receive blessings, and return to bless others. Church camps, weekend retreats, private prayer moments, and other specially focused spiritual experiences often allow us to return to the mountaintop for periods of renewal and reflection. These spiritual summits provide resting places on the journey of life. They often reconnect us to God, reminding us of the warmth and excitement of our earlier encounters. They bring back the memories and emotions of our awakening to God's forgiving grace. Sometimes, camps and retreats provide tools that will enable pilgrims to develop deeper spiritual lives and re-image their walk with God. Annual retreats, Emmaus weekends, men's/women's retreats, senior high camps, renewal conferences and so many more events rekindle a passion to serve God, though such passion is all too often short-lived. Scheduled spiritual events serve as wonderful ministries. They are often structured to bring pilgrims back to those mountaintop moments, to recover something that perhaps has been lost, to rekindle an excitement in the walk with God. The Walk to Emmaus experience is particularly focused on engaging Christians on a deeper walk with God. The 72-hour spiritual experience is skillfully crafted to invite pilgrims into safe spaces where they can reflect on their journey with God and their relationships with family, their faith community, and others. Emmaus walks, church camps, and other experiences like them provide opportunities to re-engage God on a deeper level for the purpose of growing in grace and serving others. Mountaintops provide a wonderful place to rest, enjoy the view, and be blessed by God. One can see why they are so attractive. However, with any type of mountaintop experience, there is the temptation and desire to stay and dwell, which generally undermines the purpose for the spiritual encounter. The task, admittedly a difficult one, is to embrace the lessons learned from the mountaintop and apply them in other spiritual landscapes.

Lessons Learned on the Mountain

Mountaintop experiences teach us valuable lessons of familiarity, trust, and intimacy in our relationships with God. These three flow into one another. As we become more familiar with God, we begin to develop trust, which in turn leads us toward intimacy. While these lessons can be learned in any landscape, they are more easily accessible on mountaintops. Familiarity is a vital lesson for our spiritual journey. Our ability to recognize and become comfortable in God's presence is foundational for spiritual growth. Mountains facilitate discoveries that lead us to recognize what God looks like, feels like, moves like, and sounds like to us. Mountaintop experiences serve as "thin places," to borrow a Celtic phrase. "Thin places" are those physical and metaphorical spaces where the veil between the divine and human is lifted and we can see more clearly the reflections of God. Mountaintops provide an atmosphere that stimulates familiarity, both between us and God and between us and our fellow human beings.

The Old Testament story of Samuel gives us a wonderful insight into the timeless struggle for familiarity with God. The Scripture text suggests that "the word of the Lord was rare in those days and visions were not widespread" (1 Samuel 3:1). For many reasons, the people had lost the ability to recognize the movement and voice of God. They lacked familiarity and intimacy. Within this context, a young boy, working with the high priest Eli, enters the story. Samuel assisted Eli who had grown old and weary and who did not see well. The boy slept in the tabernacle of God by the Ark of the Covenant. The Ark sat in the temple of Lord where, it was believed, God resided on earth. This was the holiest possible place for a Hebrew to be. The boy Samuel slept in the presence of God, but was unable to recognize the divine voice. One night, as Samuel was bedding down by the Ark, he heard a voice calling out his name. Assuming it was Eli, who slept in the other room, Samuel got up and went in to serve his old master. Eli informed the boy that he did not call him. The young boy heard something again as he attempted to sleep by the Ark of God, but he was unable to distinguish the voice he heard and continued to assume he was hearing the voice of Eli. Three times Samuel heard his name called but could not identify the voice of God. He needed instruction to understand that the voice he heard was that of God, who evidently wanted to have a conversation with him. Samuel physically dwelt on a metaphorical mountaintop, living by the Ark of God, and he still was unable to recognize the voice of God.[4] Eli realized it was God calling the boy and instructed Samuel how to respond because Samuel was young and had not yet come to the point where he could recognize the voice of

God. Today, numerous Christians struggle with the ability (or inability) to discern God's voice and God's will in the familiar circumstances of life. Some have been on their journeys for years and still struggle. They stand in need of assistance to recognize the movements of God in the world. The type of aid Eli gave Samuel was nothing particularly remarkable. The only instruction Eli gave to Samuel was to open himself up to the presence of God. He asked Samuel to entertain the possibility that God could be speaking to him. Ultimately, Eli helped the boy gain a greater awareness of the presence of God. "Go back and lie down; and if he calls you, you shall say, 'Speak, Lord, for your servant is listening'" (1 Samuel 3:9). There was no elaborate program or fancy instructions, only the attempt to heighten Samuel's awareness of God and the guidance to listen.

Familiarity with God, which we begin to develop on mountaintops, instills trust and allows us to become comfortable in God's presence. Perhaps most importantly, it leads us toward a greater intimacy with God. In any friendly relationship, familiarity leads to trust and to a deeper context of intimacy. Dating moves us toward a greater knowledge of one another that allows us to become more comfortable with each other. As we grow in familiarity and trust, we begin to develop intimacy that can move us from friends to lovers. Biblical images of intimacy with God often employ bride and bridegroom metaphors. "Knowing" God involves more than just intellectual acknowledgment. The term itself presents an image of intimacy. The Old Testament writers often spoke of a man "knowing" his wife, which was a sexual image. The injunction, "Be still and know that I am God!" (Psalm 46:10) involves more than just intellectual stimulation. It speaks of familiarity and intimacy. Mountaintop spiritual experiences aid us in recognizing God. They energize our pilgrimage and teach us valuable lessons of intimacy and presence, assurance and direction. Samuel's story teaches us that while we think of mountaintops as individual experiences, we still need others to help facilitate our spiritual growth. Sadly, many do not realize the priceless lessons received from mountaintop encounters. They get lost in the emotional warmth and spiritual excitement of the experience without the ability to balance the experience with the application of the mountain's lessons.

Concerns Regarding Mountaintop Spirituality

The popular expression of mountaintop spirituality can present a limited and problematic spirituality that lacks a holistic understanding of the Christian experience. Mountaintop spirituality, with its emphasis on spiritual euphoria, diminishes the value of spiritual desert and valley landscapes for the Christian experience. As a result, the rich lessons and experiences of the deserts and valleys are lost, and spirituality becomes unbalanced. Two particular issues arise and deserve exploration. First, mountaintop spirituality promotes unrealistic expectations for the Christian journey. Second, it places tremendous focus on replicating the God experience.

Unrealistic Expectations

Perhaps the greatest problem with mountaintop spirituality is the unrealistic expectations that often accompany it. Mountaintop spirituality tends to cultivate an assumption that the Christian life, rightly lived, is filled with emotional highs, spiritual energy, constant excitement, and a sustainable euphoria. While these feelings can be a wonderful part of some mountaintop encounters and remain important for spiritual growth, it is unrealistic to expect that the whole of the Christian life is a spiritual extreme. "Spiritual highs give us temporary relief," Thomas Keating suggests, "but when they subside they leave us back where we were with all the same problems."[5] This unbalanced approach leads many people on a roller coaster of emotions. As the journey turns and one travels through the unfamiliar terrains of deserts and valleys, a struggle ensues to envision God in these foreign landscapes. This often leads to a desperate confrontation between ideal Christianity and the reality of a faith crisis.

Segments of Christian teaching and preaching have reinforced an unbalanced understanding of spirituality. Messages consistently lack a healthy balanced theology that includes tools to assist pilgrims through various spiritual terrains. Too often the primary message addresses ways to return or stay on spiritual mountaintops while ignoring the question of how to walk through the desert struggles of our faith. This type of Christian spirituality presents an understanding of God that highlights blessings, exciting Christian experiences, and good living. Generally, it does not address issues surrounding individual or community faith crises, the needs of the poor, the homeless, and the hungry. A close examination of many Christian television programs reveals a self-serving Christianity. "God wants to bless you!" is often the closing line as the lights dim and the music begins. Health and wealth themes abound in Christian media, with promises of exciting, blessing-filled lives. This overly optimistic worldview leaves people ill-prepared for many of the harsh realities of the Christian life and life in general.

Christians labor to understand suffering in their lives and in the world around them. Much of American Christianity has no theology of suffering. September 11, 2001, drove this reality home to the pews of thousands of churches. The inherent unbalance of mountaintop spirituality left people anguishing with deeply rooted theological questions without any means to address them. The myopic focus on spiritual euphoria provides very little space for suffering in one's relationship with God. This absence of suffering in our concepts of God has had tremendous impact on the course of Christianity in America. Somehow, many American Christians have come to believe that God likes us best and that the material wealth of our culture is a reflection of God's blessings on capitalism, democracy, and the American way. We will continue to struggle with our concept of God if we maintain an exclusive mountaintop view of Christianity with its unrealistic expectations. Moreover, we will remain spiritually and socially ill prepared to deal with death, world hunger, injustice, war, and suffering. When Christianity is framed as mountaintop euphoria, we are left with a limited understanding of God that has little biblical or historical reference. One solution to the unrealistic expectations of mountaintop spirituality is to reclaim historical and biblical narratives, which place spiritual excitement alongside the idea of suffering as an inescapable part of life. This is the beginning of a more balanced theology. The biblical and historical narratives invite readers into the story. These narratives allow us to experience the struggles of barren women who anguished to understand themselves in a culture that defined them by bearing and caring for children. Much can be gleaned from the stories of oppression and captivity and from the struggles that people had to discover God in the midst of suffering. Various forms of liberation theologies have raised these issues. Ultimately, we must take a more serious look at the cross and pause long enough to reflect on divine suffering. It is too easy to rush from Palm Sunday to Easter without encountering the suffering of God. Without the suffering of Good Friday, we are left with a hollow Easter, praising and celebrating the resurrection while ignoring the pain of death and the suffering of God.

The deeper lessons of Passion week remind us that the journey with God is not without suffering, mystery, confusion, alongside of blessings, comfort, peace, and victory. When we come to God expecting a journey filled only with joy and excitement, we have failed to comprehend the biblical and historical revelations of God. We are left with a choice: either we walk with God through the spiritual mountains, valleys, and deserts of life, or we attempt to replicate the mountaintop spiritual experiences over and over again. And, in the process, we may fail to see God's presence in the other spiritual landscapes in which we spend so much of our time.

Reproducing the God Experience

A second difficulty that grows out of mountaintop spirituality is an attempt to replicate God experiences. Attempting to replicate our past experiences with God is often an endeavor to recapture the spiritual exhilaration that we once may have felt in an encounter with God. If we simply work to replicate our experiences of the past, then we have not only missed an opportunity for spiritual growth, but we have also misunderstood the divine lessons of the mountaintop. Spiritual maturity must move us beyond the expectation that Christian spirituality is a series of electrifying encounters isolated from the entirety of life. Christian maturity beckons us to embrace the totality of life as a journey with God, whose divine presence encompasses all of the spiritual terrains of life.

There are numerous ways in which we attempt to replicate the God experience. Perhaps corporate worship has become the most significant outlet for replicating mountaintop experiences. Worship styles, music, atmosphere, and conduct have become controversial areas inside and outside the church. According to the Isaiah chapter 6 model, worship is meant to usher us into the throne room of God. At its best, such worship is an experience of a divine/human dance with call and response, giving and receiving. Worship may well take us to the mountaintop where we bathe in the glory of God and the excitement of a divine encounter. We, like Isaiah, may stand in the temple in the presence of God as unclean people in need of cleansing and the holy touch of God. However, worship may also lead us to the desert, where we find ourselves, like Moses, communing with God in the harsh landscape of our own Mt. Sinai, struggling to understand the divine plan for our lives. Worship is a part of our continuous journey through the spiritual landscapes of life. It invigorates us to go and serve God, utilizing our spiritual gifts to spread God's love and grace. Worship, rightly formed, can provide a healthy encounter with God without simply replicating old experiences.

Conclusion

For many Christians, mountaintop spirituality needs to be re-envisioned in order to embrace its lessons and overcome its weaknesses. Mountaintop spirituality must be situated in the context of the greater sojourn in order to truly value it contributions to other terrains. A healthy mountain spirituality paradoxically embraces both the harshness and gentleness of mountain metaphors.[6] Spiritual mountains can be wilderness topographies, harsh environments that do not resemble the warm embrace that many Christians have come to expect from mountaintops. A healthy balance between images of harsh and gentle mountains has been lost by many who embrace a popular form of mountaintop spirituality. They prefer to remember the beautiful views from the summit and the much-needed rest we enjoy at the top, but they forget the struggle to ascend the mountain. They focus on the arrival while overlooking the value of the journey.

The popular form of mountaintop spirituality has highlighted the top of the mountain, but ignored the often difficult climb up and the tiring journey down. As a result, the image of the mountain as wilderness, along with the importance of the climb, has been lost to many Christians. Brian Seaward reminds us that "a mountain peak may offer itself as a metaphor of the completion of the journey, but the trip of life never ends on a mountaintop. One stays there only long enough to enjoy the view and become inspired before beginning the descent."[7] Early Church Father Gregory of Nyssa declared: "the knowledge of God is a mountain steep indeed and difficult to climb."[8] If we desire to sit at the feet of Jesus on the mountaintop, we must also experience the difficult journey to the top, for it is the journey to the top that allows us to see, understand, and comprehend the words of the Christ.

The purpose of this chapter has been to explore the strengths and weaknesses of a popular mountaintop spiritual model, while calling the reader to envision a broader spirituality that equally values spiritual valleys and deserts. Mountaintop spirituality is a wonderful place to begin a reflective relationship with God. Mountaintop moments energize us, stimulate our desire to walk with God, and have the power to transform us into new creations. Mountaintop spiritual encounters facilitate a clarity of focus and a strange familiarity with the divine. Besides the warmth and assurance that we often receive, we begin to taste what it is like to dwell mindfully in the presence of God. Familiarity, trust, and intimacy are the major lessons that we take from mountaintop encounters. These vital, life-transforming lessons are meant to be implemented in all of the spiritual terrains through which we travel. Learning to recognize and live in the presence of God is a monumental undertaking that too many Christians never seriously consider. Mountain spirituality, rightly applied, expands our knowledge and awareness of God while revealing the innermost aspects of our selves. Mountaintop encounters invite us not only to acknowledge God, but to sit and commune with God, becoming comfortable in the divine presence and tasting the sweetness of Immanuel, God with us. This is why we long to stay on the mountains and avoid the other spiritual terrains of life.

The gap between what we receive from mountaintop experiences and our ability to apply the blessings to life has continued to grow. The remainder of this book invites readers to explore and perhaps re-image the spiritual journey through the various spiritual landscapes of life. It is an invitation to discover a more balanced spirituality that opens all of life to God's movement and presence. It calls us to a deeper reflection on the implications of God's indwelling presence in our lives through Jesus Christ. Slowly, as we are able to receive the experience, God is being birthed in us, coming into a fuller reality in our lives, the unfolding of an "Incarnation Reality." Our awareness of God grows and develops as God becomes more and more of a reality to us. Conversely, we grow in our ability to live in the reality of the presence of God.

Mountaintop spirituality is a wonderful starting place for a journey with God, but it is only one landscape in our lives. As much as we may long for, mountaintops make up only a small portion of our journey. If we disregard the fact that God is just as present in spiritual deserts and valleys, we will be unable to have a fully developed relationship with God. We must remember to enjoy the mountains, embrace the spiritual warmth and rest with God, but then to return to the spiritual valleys and venture into the spiritual deserts.

Endnotes

1. Henri J. M. Nouwen, *The Path of Peace* (New York: Crossroad, 1995), 14.
2. All Scripture is quoted from the New Revised Standard Version unless otherwise indicated.
3. Belden C. Lane, *The Solace of Fierce Landscapes: Exploring Desert and Mountain Spirituality* (Oxford: Oxford University Press, 1998), 65.
4. See 1 Samuel 3 for the wonderful story of Samuel's call.
5. Thomas Keating, *Invitation to Love: The Way of Christian Contemplation* (New York: Continuum, 1994), 11.
6. See Lane, *The Solace of Fierce Landscapes*; his work is particularly helpful in the exploration of the dual nature of mountain spirituality.
7. Brain Luke Seaward, *Stand Like Mountain, Flow Like Water: Reflections on Stress and Human Spirituality* (Deerfield Beach, Fla.: Health Communications, 1997), 56.
8. Gregory of Nyssa, *The Life of Moses*, vol. 2, 58, trans. Abraham J. Malherbe and Everett Ferguson, Cistercian Studies 31 (New York: Paulist, 1978), 93.

3
Mountaintop Spirituality 2
A Mountaintop Perspective of Deserts and Valleys

The popularity of mountaintop spirituality necessitates further investigation of its impact on spiritual deserts and valleys. Chapter two presented the value and importance of mountaintop spirituality for our spiritual formation and pointed out a few very important problems that distract us from a more holistic spirituality. This chapter explores specific implications that an exclusively mountaintop spirituality can have on our understanding of spiritual deserts and valleys. Our desire for mountaintop moments can easily skew our overall perspective on the Christian journey. Deserts and valleys, however, have valuable lessons to teach us about ourselves and God, lessons that cannot be learned on mountaintops; and if we ignore these landscapes, we will struggle to understand the movement of God in the world around us. Valley and desert terrains provide some essential insights into the experience of the sacred in the ordinary. They also offer some ways to find God's presence through struggle.

The popular mountaintop spirituality of our culture tends to view spiritual deserts as terrains of abandonment where one is punished for sins, rather than places of divine hiddenness and potential spiritual growth.

Spiritual valleys are generally ignored or consigned to obscurity by our desire to dwell on spiritual summits. This spawns disdainful attitudes toward the valley as simply a transitional landscape. Contrasting common misconceptions of deserts and valleys with alternative understandings offers us healthy options to a more holistic spirituality.

Spiritual Deserts

One of the great tragedies of an exclusively mountaintop spiritual perspective is the loss of the desert as sacred place. Spiritual deserts play an important role in our spiritual journeys. If they are avoided or portrayed as places of divine abandonment or punishment, our spiritual formation could be jeopardized. Today, popular spirituality often avoids the desert for more comfortable landscapes that reinforce unexamined spirituality. The examination of our faith and reflections on our spiritual journeys can lead us to the edge of a spiritual desert, releasing a flood of emotions from fear to confusion. This is a primary reason why Christians desire to avoid deserts. Spiritual deserts are sacred places to struggle with God, ourselves, and life itself. Deserts are valuable teachers that can aid us in contemplating the deeper questions of our faith while calling us inward and downward to a profound place with God. The journey through spiritual deserts is often hostile to that which we have come to call Christianity. Deserts tear away at the things we hold most dear while beckoning us to a deeper understanding of sacred space.

For many, the desert remains a place to be avoided because it lacks the luster of a mountaintop atmosphere that one comes to associate with God's presence. In addition, there is a deep-seated, perhaps unconscious fear that our preconceived notions and dominant paradigms of religiosity cannot survive the journey from death to life that the desert demands of its pilgrims. In short, we are afraid that we may lose the form of Christianity that we have worked so hard to construct, that God may escape from the box in which we have conveniently placed the Divine. We are afraid that the demands of the desert will strip away the superficialities of our religious experiences and leave us confused, lonely, and lost in a hostile terrain. Ironically, our spiritual journeys are often characterized by desert experiences, leading us to dwell in the very places we most fear and try to avoid.

The popular mountaintop perspective tends to place an opposition between spiritual deserts and the highs of spiritual mountains. Historically and biblically, deserts have been places of struggle with God and ourselves. Many American Protestants have been taught, by well-meaning people, to fear spiritual deserts and the personal faith crises that often accompany them. Desert experiences can shake the very foundation of one's theology, leaving the sojourner with a feeling of confusion, loneliness, and searching. It is easy to discover why spiritual deserts are often portrayed as landscapes to be avoided, places of abandonment, punishment, and even death. Spiritual deserts, properly perceived, place Christians in particular tensions: abandonment or hiddenness, punishment or growth, death or a new understanding of life. The value of deserts is lost when only one side of the tension—abandonment, punishment, and death—is highlighted, leaving us with a skewed understanding of God and a foggy lens through which to read Scripture.

Abandonment or Hiddenness

One tension of the desert lies between sensations of divine abandonment and the hiddenness of God. Fear of abandonment—of being left alone, unloved, or isolated—is a basic human fear. Children certainly face this fear; however, as adults we mask or even deny it. How does one determine the difference between being abandoned by God and experiencing the hiddenness of God? The assurance of God's presence is affirmed in Psalm 139, which insists that there is no escaping God's watchful eye. However, the feeling of abandonment can be strong. It is often difficult to move beyond the deeply rooted emotion of being forsaken to embrace divine assurance. The psalmists struggled with this tension. "My God, my God, why have you forsaken me? Why are you so far from helping me, from the words of my groaning. O my God, I cry by day, but you do not answer; by night, but find no rest" (Psalm 22:1-2). Is God only present when we "feel" divine closeness, or is it possible that intense emotions mask our perception of God? Our deep desires for the divine intimacy associated with mountaintop experiences, coupled with our lack of awareness of God, lead us to conclude that we have been abandoned by God when we enter a spiritual desert. There, left to struggle alone, we lament with the words of the psalmist, "How long will you forget me? How long will you hide your face from me?" (Psalm 13:1).

The hiddenness of God is one of the most difficult elements of the spiritual journey. The psalmist reflected this struggle by asking, "Why O Lord do you stand far off? Why do you hide yourself in times of trouble?" (Psalm 10:1). We agonize, trying to understand why God would hide from a seeking heart. "The purpose for God's apparent absence, of God's hiding," Belden Lane observed, "is to deepen in the lover a longing for the one loved, to enhance the joy experienced when fear dissolves and the separated are rejoined."[1] Sometimes we get so caught up in the business of life, the pursuit of careers, and a number of other things that we start to ignore our relationship with God. It is often when we begin experiencing a strange sense of absence that we begin a desperate search for God.

My son Grant learned this lesson when he was about three years old. The family was shopping at the mall, and I was watching Grant as my wife and daughter went to shop for something. A three-year-old has little patience for random browsing in a mall, so I let him take the lead and watched him experience the place, people, sights, and sounds of this strange environment. As an over-protective father, I never let my children get far from me, especially in large public areas. I walked slowly behind Grant as he explored and, occasionally, attempted to wander off. I had warned him against going too far away from me, but a three-year-old has a hard time distinguishing between far enough and too far. So, I watched him as he continued to express his freedom and go a little farther from me. He went into a toy store to play with a display of wooden trains while I remained by the door. He continued to keep watch for my presence at first. But, as he became more and more comfortable with his newfound freedom, his attention turned to other things. I positioned myself in a new location to watch him without his knowledge. I could see the joy on his face as he joined other small children playing with a toy train display. After several minutes of pleasurable playing, he turned to look for me and discovered that I was gone from his sight. At first his look was curious. I am sure he thought, "Dad would never abandon me." Nevertheless, Dad was not within view. Slowly, he stopped his playing and began to turn his attention to finding me. He stood by the display at first and turned in all directions without seeing me. Then his face began to change, expressing worry, panic, fear, and terror that he might be lost or abandoned. As his silent tears began to flow down his face, I could no longer remain hidden. I could not bear the pain that I was causing him and myself. I knew he was not lost nor abandoned. He did not. I could see him and keep him from harm the entire time. At any point I could have revealed myself and he would have continued playing; but when he thought he was lost, the playing stopped and the seeking began. When he saw me, he ran to embrace me as tightly as he could. We exchanged "I love you's," as I picked him up and carried him. As I recall, he fell asleep on my shoulder as we left the mall and walked to the car.

Similarly God is sometimes hidden, but never lost. God stands with us as we play, suffer, struggle, wander, love, discover, explore, and seek. God's desire for intimacy with us never changes. Life just distracts us. The spiritual deserts in our lives have a way of getting our attention. We too often take God's presence for granted, not because of some deep mystical awareness, but because we think we have conveniently located God in a place that we can continue to return to when we need something. Much to our surprise, we look to discover that God is not there. Panic, fear, terror, and confusion set in as we begin a desperate search for a God who, we believe, has abandoned us. But we also know the joy of being found and the warmth of being picked up and carried. We long to fall asleep on God's shoulder, to find divine rest, to be embraced in the arms of God. God is sometimes hidden, but never lost. If we envision the desert as spiritual abandonment or as an exile from the mountaintop, we will miss the importance of seeking and the lessons of discovery.

Punishment or Growth

Along with divine abandonment, spiritual deserts are often understood as places of punishment for those who are disobedient. If one envisions Christianity as a series of mountaintop encounters, then spiritual deserts could be easily understood as divine punishment. However, it is our lack of awareness of God's presence and our unbalanced spirituality that lead us to equate spiritual deserts with divine punishment. The Exodus account is often employed to support our notions that the desert is a place of divine punishment. After the Israelites' refusal to cross into the Promised Land, due to the fearful report of ten out of twelve spies, God commanded that they roam in the wilderness (the Sinai Peninsula) for forty years until all people over the age of twenty had died.[2] This punishment was a result of years of rebellion and rejection, despite God's attempts to draw the people close. While God never abandoned the Israelites during their desert sojourn, for a generation the desert became a place of wandering, death, and destruction. However, the desert drew Moses closer to God and provided an environment for a new generation of Israelites to learn trust and dependence.

While some utilize the Exodus story to affirm desert experiences as divine punishment, they ignore countless Scriptures that represent the desert as a place of spiritual growth and clarity. Biblical and historical narratives consistently portray the Spirit of God leading people into the desert, where they struggle with God and themselves. The Israelites, Elijah, John the Baptist, Jesus, St. Antony, and Amma Theodora all give testimony to the divine call into the wilderness. Jesus was driven into the desert by the Spirit of God after his baptism (Matthew 4:1, Mark 1:12, Luke 4:1). The desert provided a space for him to struggle with questions of meaning, purpose, identity, and the temptations of life. Jesus experienced those struggles of the desert, emerging from it, empowered by the Spirit of the Lord, preaching the good news, proclaiming freedom and recovery of sight, and beginning a ministry of sharing his life and insights into God with others (Luke 4:18-19). He emerged in the power of the Spirit to show others the way to live out a life in union with God.

Spiritual deserts can be wonderful places of rich spiritual growth. They are places of transformation for those who are far away from God as well as those who are near. The desert demands that we stand transparent, vulnerable, authentic, and naked before God. We can hide nothing. We can demand nothing. We can give nothing. It is from this place that growth begins. God leads us into deserts, not as a punishment, but as a place of clarity, leading to blessings. God desires intimacy with us, an intimacy that flows from grace. Spiritual deserts facilitate this divine dance. God beckons us to come and dance as the music moves from disco to waltz. God stands before us with hand extended, calling us out on the dance floor, prepared to embrace the mood of the music. God's question is, "Do you want to dance?"

When approached with a deep sense of authenticity, the desert leads us into deeper places with God—places where we struggle with the hard realities of life and places where God calls us to "grow up," or perhaps I should say "grow down," to plumb the depths of the Christian experience.

Thomas Keating said, "At some point in our spiritual growth Jesus asks us to adjust ourselves to a new relationship with himself. Since this happens without much warning, almost no one has any awareness of what is taking place when it actually happens."³ At some point in time, God calls us to move from the faith of our childhood to that of an adult. In the crisis of the desert experience we often "reach for our God image, the one we left hidden in the recesses of our memory."⁴ However, our image of God may have become irrelevant to our present situation because it depends too much on visions from childhood or pop psychology. "Recollecting this inappropriate and inadequate image, people will sometimes reject God entirely instead of pondering how God might look through the eyes of a mature adult."⁵ Henri Nouwen referred to this childhood state as the "magical" stage of spirituality, one that allows God to remain "the magical pacifier whose existence depends on ours."⁶

The call to Christian maturity is not easy to receive or to respond to. A supportive community of faith is vital for the desert sojourn. The desert confronts us with our unbalanced spirituality, often leaving us confused and hurting. Faith communities can offer encouragement and spiritual direction to navigate the landscape. "God goes after our accumulated junk and starts digging through our defense mechanisms," as we travel through deserts "revealing the secret corners that hide the unacceptable parts of ourselves. We may think it is the end of our relationship with God. Actually, it is an invitation to a new depth of relationship with God."⁷ This is a truth we discover on our sojourn through the desert wilderness.

Spiritual deserts are difficult but necessary places for our sojourn. Our experiences in these holy and harsh places are often complicated by the fact that we receive little information and guidance. Furthermore, most of what we do receive reinforces the idea that the desert is a place of abandonment and punishment.

Spiritual deserts scarcely rival mountaintop spirituality. Who among us would prefer the harshness of the desert to the embrace of the mountain? Although it is not a question of preference, it is an issue of awareness and perspective. We *will* encounter spiritual deserts on our journey with God through life, so we need to get a better understanding of the desert landscape and improve our ability to respond to it in appropriate ways.

Will we allow our desire and the allure of spiritual mountaintops to lead us toward an unbalanced relationship with God, or will we embrace

33

an awareness of the desert as a sacred place to encounter God in a different, yet holy, way? This is the road less traveled, one that leads to a deep experience with God, and few will find it.

Spiritual Valleys

We have probed the effects of mountaintop spirituality on spiritual deserts. Now we need to explore its impact on valley spirituality. Spiritual valleys are perhaps the most overlooked, devalued, and ignored landscapes on our spiritual journey. Valleys are primarily the places where we are born, where we live, where we grow, and where we die. They are actually the dominant landscapes of our lives. We may visit mountains or deserts, but we generally live in the valleys, plains, marshes, and flat places at the foot of mountains or the edges of deserts. Our perception of valleys, both spiritual and physical, can easily drift toward the ordinary, the mundane, or the normal. Too many people thoughtlessly dismiss spiritual valleys as transitional landscapes that are not intended for habitation.

Mountaintop spirituality can disturb our desire and, possibly, even our capacity to dwell in spiritual valleys. Some never even entertain the possibility of being valley dwellers or exploring their spirituality in the common and ordinary. The purpose here is to reveal how a spirituality based on mountaintop encounters assigns spiritual valleys to the regions of the mundane, the lukewarm, and the indifferent. The Book of Revelation suggests that it is better to be hot or cold than lukewarm, for God hates the mediocrity of indecision (Revelation 3:16). However, one should not be so quick to define spiritual valleys as places of indecision and mediocrity. Valleys can be fertile locations where we plant, nurture, and grow our relationship with God; but like other terrains, spiritual valleys are filled with tensions.

Two tensions are particularly present in spiritual valleys. The first tension involves the question of whether the valley is a transitional place through which one passes or a dwelling place in which one lives. A second tension exists with one's attitude toward the valley. We often struggle with complacency in spiritual valleys; we feel stuck in the mundane. This, however, leads us to ignore the simple and ordinary expressions of God in the world around us. A complacent attitude lacks the intentionality required to see the ordinary as sacred space that is filled with the simple acts of God.

Passing Through Or Dwelling Place?

If we perceive our spiritual journey as a series of mountaintop experiences, then spiritual valleys become little more than fog-filled, low-lying areas that one would hope to move through quickly on the way to ascending the mountain. Valleys are easily traveled. They do not require the same effort to cross or stimulate the same emotions that occur when we travel through a desert or climb a mountain. Consciously and subconsciously, spiritual valleys become transitional landscapes that we encounter on the way to other terrains. We often respond to spiritual valleys like children on vacation, who ignore the beauty of the surroundings and ask, "Are we there yet?" That question indicates that arriving at the destination is the only thing of importance. It implies that the journey is irrelevant, except as a means, often an irritating means, to achieving our goal of arriving. The trip is simply a transition that takes us from one place to another. I remember family vacations when we drove from St. Louis to the beautiful Rocky Mountains of Colorado. Towering mountains, such as Pike's Peak, which ascends some 14,000 feet, were fascinating to a child who grew up in the Mississippi River Valley. However, before we could arrive at the foot of the Rocky Mountains, we had to cross the state of Kansas. Later in life, I lived in Olathe, Kansas, so I do not want to seem negative about the beauty of the Sunflower state; but the drive across the state of Kansas into the eastern plateaus of Colorado seemed to last forever. A child could only take so much of the never-ending fields of wheat and corn before longing for visual variety. "Are we there yet?" became a frequent question. The valley had simply become a transitional landscape by which we would arrive at the mountains. As a child, I completely ignored the beauty of the wheat fields and the value of the valley for my fascination with the mountains. The ordinary simply slipped into obscurity, taking along with it any hope of discovering the sacred in the ordinary, the holy in the common, or the divine in the simple.

Transitions, passing from one stage or place to another, are often accompanied by stress, confusion, uncertainty, and discomfort. During transitions we frequently focus on the past or the future, but rarely the present. We look back where we came from and take joy in our memories, or look forward with excitement to new adventures and opportunities that await us. Either way, we tend to ignore the present. This is a major spiritual obstacle to overcome if we hope to thrive as valley dwellers.[8]

Growing up in traditions where verbal testimonies were a regular part of a worship service, I learned very quickly that Christians spoke either about their past experiences with God or their hopes for heaven in the future more than they spoke of the present reality of God's indwelling presence. Testimonies were given with passion, love, and intensity. It was easy to get caught in the exciting stories of the transforming power of God and the wonderful miraculous things that had happened. However, it was disappointing when I realized that many of these stories were the same testimonies that had been given for the last twenty years. I found it sad to see that the reality of God was locked into experiences that were twenty years old or more. These testimonies often ended with a deep desire to encounter God once again in the same dramatic fashion. Looking back, I realize that spiritual valleys were not perceived as places to dwell and grow with God. They were simply imaged as transitional wastelands, perhaps even spiritual deserts, that lay between the person and the mountain where God dwelt. The God of the now, the present, the moment, seemed absent from so many stories of faith, so people were left to hope in a heavenly future and were in large measure deprived of the precious gifts of the present.

It is easy to see why so many Christians struggle for happiness and the discernment of God's will for their lives, to know which path to walk and how to listen to the voice of God. Our desire to be someplace else, to have another position at work, more money, or some other objects, real or imagined, keeps us from embracing the present reality of God. From a mountaintop perspective, the valley has little spiritual value to offer us on our sojourn. We can easily miss the beauty of the ordinary and perceive spiritual valleys as mysterious and vulnerable places to traverse quickly. If we are determined to perceive God solely as a mountaintop deity, then we are destined to spend much of our spiritual journey depressed, lonely, and struggling to discover a God who is and has been right beside us the entire time. We will continue to search for something that has always been near. The valley offers us a place to establish communities and develop relationships. It is a dwelling place that invites us to live, work, play, and grow in a nurturing environment that sustains us through life.

Attitude

Our attitude determines whether we approach spiritual valleys as transitional places or dwelling places. Popular images of spiritual valleys have too often been formed from a mountaintop perspective. "The valley of the shadow of death" is a likely image that fills our minds when we think of spiritual valleys (Psalm 23:4). Perhaps Ezekiel's story of the "Valley of Dry Bones" comes to mind with its images of a bone-filled basin from past battles (Ezekiel 37). Maybe we imagine apocalyptic images of the five valleys of Megiddo and the battle of Armageddon (Revelation 16:16). While all of these are valid biblical images of valleys, they only reflect one perspective in Scripture. The Bible also paints images of lush green valleys, bountiful vineyards, the mystical garden of Eden, and the fertile valleys of the Jordan. A mountaintop perspective makes it easy to view spiritual valleys as complacent landscapes. It fosters an attitude that valleys are reserved for the spiritually exhausted and those lacking the energy to climb one more mountain. So want-to-be mountaintop dwellers simply capitulate to the valley, relinquishing their quest for spiritual euphoria and settle into a spiritual poverty and depression that they believe spiritual valleys offer. This attitude is destructive because it fails to recognize the valley as sacred space.

The attitude that we bring to anything in life will largely determine the type of experience we will have. If we choose to see the valley as a refuge for the weary, the valley will serve simply as a transitional landscape; however, if we embrace the valley as a sacred place in which God is ever present, it will become our spiritual home.

A few summers ago I was reminded of the connection between attitude and experience while visiting the Painted Desert National Park in Arizona. For years, I had longed to visit the Painted Desert and watch the beauty of the landscape as the movement of the sun transformed the colors of the rocks. While sitting with my wife on a bench overlooking a canyon, I overheard a person lament, "When are we leaving here? There is nothing here but rocks and dirt!" While I was captivated with the changing colors of the "rocks and dirt" as the sun was beginning to set, another person saw nothing of beauty and longed to be freed from the experience. The attitude and perspective that I brought to the experience greatly enhanced the sacredness of the moment, while another person obviously did not perceive anything beautiful, let alone sacred. The individual's attitude may have been influenced by numerous events and circumstances of that day of which I had no knowledge; however, the fact remains that our attitude affects our experiences.

Conclusion

Whether intentional or not, mountaintop spirituality can cast a negative shadow over spiritual deserts and valleys. Earlier sections of this chapter highlighted a few problems that can grow out of an exclusively mountaintop perspective and offered hints that can lead toward a more balanced spirituality. Mountaintop experiences often blind us to God's expressions in other spiritual landscapes of life and, in the process, can rob us of a healthier more holistic spirituality. Our desire to be close to God, to experience the warmth and assurance of mountaintop moments, can overwhelm us. Spirituality, much like love, moves in and through various phases, all of which are important to a developing relationship. "Puppy love" is intense but shallow. Later, love is still intense, but we hope it is deeper. Falling in love overwhelms us with emotions and excitement to the point that we are often unable to see beyond the best parts of the one adored. We become consumed by love and all the wonderful things that revolve around it. It has been said that love is blind. The same may be said of many mountaintop Christians who live exclusively in the excitement of the moment.

The following chapters will explore in greater detail spiritual deserts and valleys and the important contributions they each have to offer us. Each landscape has valuable lessons to contribute to a holistic and healthy spirituality. When combined, mountain, valley, and desert metaphors present a spirituality that can assist us through all of life's circumstances. The landscapes invite us to journey with God through intense struggles of spiritual deserts, to climb mountains to rest and be blessed, and to dwell in the valleys wherein the ordinary reveals the sacred.

Endnotes

1. Belden Lane, *The Solace of Fierce Landscapes: Exploring Desert and Mountain Spirituality* (Oxford: Oxford University Press, 1998), 178.
2. See Numbers 14 and Deuteronomy 1–2 for detailed accounts of the refusal to enter into the Promise Land.
3. Thomas Keating, *Crisis of Faith, Crisis of Love* (New York: Continuum, 2000), 11.
4. Carol Ochs and Kerry Olitzky, *Jewish Spiritual Guidance: Finding Our Way to God* (San Francisco: Jossey-Bass, 1997), 24.
5. Ibid.
6. Henri J. M. Nouwen, *Intimacy* (San Francisco: Harper, 1969); see chapter 1: "From Magic to Faith," 5–20.
7. Thomas Keating, *Invitation To Love: The Way of Christian Contemplation* (New York: Continuum, 2000), 17.
8. Spencer Johnson wrote a wonderful little book that called attention to the "precious present." Spencer Johnson, *The Precious Present* (New York: Doubleday, 1984).

4

The Spiritual Desert as Sacred Place

Of the three landscape metaphors discussed in this book, the spiritual desert is perhaps the most difficult to navigate. Belden Lane suggests,

> The desert as metaphor is that uncharted terrain beyond the edges of the seemingly secure and structured world in which we take such confidence, a world of affluence and order we cannot imagine ever ending. Yet it does. And at the point where the world begins to crack, where brokenness and disorientation suddenly overtake us, there we step into the wide, silent plains of a desert we had never known existed.[1]

Spiritual deserts are realities for most Christians at some point on the spiritual journey. As much as we attempt to avoid desert landscapes, we often find ourselves in the places where brokenness and disorientation overtake us. We all have periods when we feel lost or confused, when we roam around in search of God. There are times when worship is empty and our prayers do not seem to make it past the ceiling. Because spiritual deserts are difficult landscapes to navigate, most people try to avoid them. However, the desert beckons us to deeper and more transparent places beyond our self-centeredness and arrogance. Spiritual deserts facilitate clarity of mind and heart, although the path to clarity is often negotiated through struggle. Desert struggles reveal the spiritual baggage that we insist on carrying, baggage that impedes our ability to hear God's call to receive grace. Periods of struggle, however, can move us to new levels of integration of our faith and allow freshness and transformation into our relationship with God and others.[2] Desert spiritual landscapes are important and vital parts of the Christian journey because they strip away the artificial aspects of our lives and require us to be authentic. They are sacred places that require reflection and provide greater insight into God.

This chapter speaks particularly to those who find themselves in spiritual deserts, willingly or unwillingly. Desert experiences can be terrifying, especially if it is an initial experience. Most of us have received very little preparation for these spiritually dry periods of our lives, and what we do know comes from watching others struggle with their faith. This tends to generate fear within us and reinforces our resolve to avoid the desert. Many of our traditions frequently add to the anguish of spiritual deserts by ignoring them altogether. We are given little help and few tools to aid us on our desert sojourns leaving us unprepared for the traumas that occur in life. Esther de Waal suggests that the journey through the desert will be costly and involve risks. It probably will not follow a clear-cut pattern with some definite end or goal in view. The really significant journey is the interior journey.[3] Spiritual deserts are going to occur in our lives, whether we seek them or not. So it is vital to address the dynamics of spiritual deserts, struggle with its demands, and embrace the lessons it offers. Some people have found the desert to be a sacred and desirable place to discover more about who God is and who we are. It is a place that summons seekers and spiritualists, mystics and monks, the cautious and the curious to wrestle with God and self. For others, the desert represents separation from God and wayward wandering that is counter-productive to the Christian's spiritual journey.

Dynamics of Desert Spirituality

The first steps into spiritual deserts are frightening ones for most Christians because everything about them is foreign. The initial panic that we experience is generated from our fear that we have lost control and will be unable to regain it. Disorientation follows closely on the heels of our fears and we are easily overtaken by the desert experience without ever realizing or embracing the richness it has to offer. Desert disorientation is magnified by experiences of emptiness, confusion, fear, anger, guilt, feelings of abandonment, and loss of passion for God. These are common desert dynamics.

Generally, we are confused by the desert dynamics. The more we travel into the hidden places of our souls, the more intense the struggle. In deserts, our spiritual lives often become dry and empty. Prayer and Scripture hold little or no meaning. Attending religious services—if, indeed, we do so—is more about appearance and going through motions than encountering God. As we wrestle with the deeper questions of our faith, we may struggle with our traditions and the teachings of our elders. Our spiritual desert experiences are often magnified by alienation from our friends, family, and communities of faith. We are afraid to talk about our feelings and thoughts because those around us are not always ready to receive our questions and doubts. They suspect that our spiritual desert is evidence of a wayward or rebellious journey. The lack of understanding that flows from our friends and families acts as an additional source of our pain.

Desert disorientation is a sensation that grows from our loss of control and our lack of awareness of God's presence in the world around us. Normally, we spend very little time reflecting on our journey through life. Apart from a tragedy or crisis in life that demands our reflection, we ignore the need to sit, be still, and think about our journey. We have lost a greater awareness of God and neglected the art of spiritual reflection. Many no longer have the ability or the desire to sit with God and reflect on life's experiences. Reflection requires a certain level of intentionality to process our journey with God through life. The issue is not God's presence, which is a constant, but our spiritual sensitivity, which may lack both an awareness of God's presence and a desire to encounter God in deeper ways. As a result, disorientation quickly overtakes us and we get lost in the desert.

We often lack the ability to name the experience through which we walk. The desert inspires intense emotions that are ever present, yet we remain uncertain of the source of these powerful feelings. Out of fear or embarrassment, we pretend that life is well. Unsure of where to find help, we continue to suffer in silence, pursue unfulfilled spiritual lives, and listen to the voices of those around us, calling in different directions. Spiritual deserts have ways of muffling those voices. Indeed, God may call us to the desert, far from the din of so many voices, so that we can hear his voice. Desert Fathers and Mothers sought out physical deserts in order to "quiet the inner noise that kept them from hearing the whispers of God."[4] The same may be said for spiritual deserts, where the many voices of life fall away, leaving only silence, which is the language of God. Spiritual deserts prepare us to hear and listen to the voice of God and to filter the noise of life that captures our attention and drowns out God's voice.

When we arrive in the desert, we are faced with the reality of place, the fear of the unknown, and the overwhelming flood of emotions that flow through our hearts and minds as we realize we have lost control of our environment. The desert experience magnifies our sensations of loss: loss of control, loss of passion, and loss of hope. We begin to echo the words of the Psalmist, "There is no help for you in God" (Psalm 3:2), or the lament of Psalm 13 that begins, "How long, O Lord? Will you forget me, forever? How long will you hide your face from me?" These words are echoed in spiritual deserts, words that reflect the disorientation that is so characteristic of such harsh terrain. Walter Brueggemann appropriately calls these Psalms "disorientation Psalms."[5] These lamentations from the Psalmist still resonate with us. The Psalmist captured some of the tendencies that flow out of spiritual desert experiences: abandonment, disorientation, fear, anger, confusion, and loss. The confusion we experience hits us as soon as we realize we have entered unfamiliar territory, a territory especially hostile to a novice. The next flood of emotion varies, depending on our personality, the way we entered into the desert, and our spiritual depth. Some become angry very quickly, both at those around them and at God. This can be especially true of those who enter the desert through a crisis in life. Others retreat into themselves. They struggle quietly with thoughts of abandonment and loss. Their feelings of loneliness and despair often lead to depression. As these emotions germinate, the deeper struggle of the spiritual desert begins.

Fear, anger, confusion, loss, and disorientation stand in stark contrast to the reassuring feelings of mountaintop spirituality, which is characterized by intimacy, embrace, assurance, and divine presence. Theologies built around mountaintop experiences emphasize an intense sense of God's presence. This leads many to believe that God has abandoned them as they travel through the desert; however, spiritual deserts can also lead to an intense awareness of God's presence. Unfortunately, we have not been taught to recognize or embrace the intimacy of spiritual deserts. As a result of our lack of knowledge, spiritual deserts become places where we are more likely to perceive the abandonment of God than to embrace intimacy with God. We are more likely to believe that we have "lost our salvation," or have "fallen away from God," than we are to see the desert as a sacred place to walk with God.

Spiritual deserts are paradoxical places that involve struggle and joy. Amma Syncletica, a fourth-century Desert Mother, said of the desert experience:

> In the beginning there are a great many battles and a good deal of suffering for those who are advancing towards God and afterwards, ineffable joy. It is like those who wish to light a fire; at first they are choked by the smoke and cry, and by this means obtain what they seek so we also must kindle the divine fire in ourselves through tears and hard work.[6]

She beautifully described the tension of spiritual deserts between struggle and reward. Thomas Keating described the awakening of the desert sojourn:

> At some point in our journey, a pervasive sense of God's absence begins to manifest itself during prayer and spreads into other areas of one's life. This is actually the beginning of a deeper union with Christ. Most of us, however, do not experience it that way. When the biblical desert opens up within us, we worry that something is going wrong in our relationship with God . . . we are called to make a transition from superficial spiritual nourishment to the solid food of pure faith.[7]

Both Amma Syncletica and Thomas Keating understand that the desert is a place of great struggle and great blessing. It is a place of spiritual growth via the path of struggle.

The desert journey is a painful one because it strips away a naive and unexamined faith. Spiritual deserts strip us of the artificial and move us toward the authentic. We all struggle with authentic reflections, understanding the true nature of who we are. Each of us posture a "false self" to some degree. The "false self" is simply an image of who we want others to believe that we are. At some point we even begin to believe the image that we try so hard to project. This image, however, has been constructed apart from the reality of who we truly are in God. The desert spiritual journey reveals our attempts to build up a "false self," and to hide our woundedness from ourselves, others, and God. The spiritual desert invites us to envision God in ways that provide healing for our woundedness and enable us to perceive life with a clarity that will lead us to know who we truly are, to be our "transparent self."

Entering the Desert

How do we get into spiritual deserts, these largely mysterious and harsh landscapes? Most of us never really anticipate entering desert spiritual terrains. Generally, we just try to avoid them. Once we realize that we have indeed entered a spiritual desert, we begin to rehearse a series of questions: Why am I in a desert? What did I do to deserve this? How can I get out of here? Where is God in all of this? These questions reflect our confusion, fears, and lack of control. Knowing how we arrive in spiritual deserts is important to our understanding of their deeper meaning and purpose. There are two major ways that we enter into desert spiritual experiences. First, crises in our lives can bring us to the heart of spiritual deserts. Crises cause us to become reflective, and reflection begins to awaken us to the reality of our spiritual journey and life around us. Second, God has historically led pilgrims directly into the desert experience. Moses, Elijah, John the Baptist, Jesus, and the Desert Fathers and Mothers all felt divine direction to enter into a desert spiritual experience.

Whether we enter spiritual deserts through God's leading, stumble into them as a result of life crises, or simply drift into the desert through neglect of our relationship with God, we often find ourselves reflecting on serious questions about our faith, our God, and ourselves. Our first questions in the desert are generally self-centered and loaded with emotional intensity.

Initially, we are more concerned with the loss of control of our lives than with exploring intimacy with God in the desert environment. Our initial responses to spiritual deserts—confusion, fear, loss, even anger—distract us from a focus on divine intimacy. However, the desert can become a sacred place for us as we struggle with God and ourselves.

Crisis

Crises often bring us to the unfamiliar desert terrain, landscapes devoid of lush green meadows and the warm emotions we have come to associate with our encounters with God. We may arrive in spiritual deserts by way of broken relationships, death of loved ones, loss of employment, divorce, long- and short-term illnesses, or numerous other situations, all of which can challenge the very foundations of our faith. These crises are often accompanied by feelings of loss, fear, anger, abandonment, and loneliness, which rise to the surface and become unwelcome companions on our journey through the desert. Life's crises stimulate deeper questions and struggles that we have perhaps hidden from ourselves and others. During crises, old baggage often resurfaces, and we are faced with the past and the memories that it stimulates.

During a crisis we are confronted with life as it really is, not as we want it to be. We are awakened to the stark reality of life and our inability to control our circumstances. This, in turn, often leads us to a point of spiritual reflection. We begin to reach for God with a new intentionality. Some rest in their faith and try to ride out the storm generated by a crisis, while others dust off the box in which God has been placed and begin the process of reflection. Crisis facilitates reflection and reflection is a vital part of spiritual growth. If crisis is the vehicle, reflection is the path that transports us to spiritual deserts where we often stand without those things that both distract us and allow us to remain superficial. Crisis stimulates difficult questions about our lives and our relationship with God and others, while demanding authentic responses. The desert penetrates us to the heart of our being, releasing questions and emotions from a place deep within that we had forgotten was there. As the secret places in our hearts slowly start to open with all of the pain from the wounds of the past, we reluctantly take our first steps into the desert.

Crises have the potential to bring us closer to God, reveal our heart, and help us engage God and others more honestly. However, crises also have the potential to push us away from God and complicate our relationships with others. It is a tension. The more we fight the changing spiritual terrain, the more difficult it is to embrace God and the lessons of the desert. Eventually, we either capitulate and fall into the holy ambiguity and mystery of the spiritual desert or we continue to fight against the experience. At some point, we may want to turn around and run back to the safety of an unexamined faith. At its best, the desert is a place of divine intimacy. It calls us to struggle with the essence of ourselves and be transformed by God's grace. At its worst, the desert is a place of destruction. Some are unable to navigate the spiritual desert and become lost in the suffering. Instead of becoming a sacred place to encounter God, it becomes a destructive terrain. The reality of the desert is that life can be discovered or life can be lost.

There are many stories of desert spiritual struggles and the faith crises that they stimulate. Kathy and Matt's story of a family dealing with cancer reflects two different ways people dealt with spiritual deserts. A few years ago, while I was serving as a United Methodist pastor, a member of the Church was diagnosed with breast cancer. Kathy was in her forties, with two school-aged daughters and a loving husband. The family was a regular part of congregational life, involved in youth group, Bible School, Summer Camp, and other programs. I did not really know them well before the diagnosis. After the initial shock was over and the course of treatment was determined, Kathy arranged a time to talk with me. We had talked several times, but hospital visits are not always the best environments for deep conversations. I had traveled this path with families before and I knew something about the pain and struggles that would lie ahead. I anticipated a conversation that would focus on hard theological questions about God and suffering. I was surprised to encounter an individual who was deeply rooted in her faith in God and understood the desert as a sacred place. She had experienced her personal desert two years before with the death of her mother from breast cancer. Kathy had struggled with her understanding of God and suffering as she watched her mother dying. Our time together was spent talking about the faith crisis and spiritual desert that her husband Matt was going through. The news of breast cancer had caused him to raise a number of serious questions about God and about his Christianity.

47

Like many people in crisis, he asked mostly self-centered questions, "why" questions which are always impossible to answer and are usually destructive for the inquirer. According to Kathy, Matt's religious experiences were never really deep. He had enjoyed the friendships they had built at the church over the years, and recently he had started to seek more spiritual guidance for his life. Kathy's cancer became his spiritual desert.

During one of Kathy's treatments, Matt and I had time to talk during lunch at the hospital. I let him lead the conversation and explore whatever topics he wanted. I was not sure if Kathy had spoken to him about our earlier conversation. After some small talk, Matt dropped the bomb. "Why do you think God causes or allows people to suffer? Kathy is a godly woman. She loves our kids, cares for me, and is one of the best examples of a Christian I know. How can God let this happen to her? You know, her mother died of breast cancer. It was a horrible way to die. Do you think God answers prayers of godly people? What about healing? Does God still do that?" Matt knew I did not have the answers to all of his questions. In reality, he did not intend for me to answer them. What was clear was that Matt had arrived in a spiritual desert via Kathy's breast cancer. His casual search for God before the cancer was transformed into a desperate pursuit. Matt stood face to face with a situation he could not control, and God seemed like the only one who might be able to help. However, he was uncertain that God was not, somehow, the cause of suffering. Kathy's breast cancer became the crisis that caused Matt to enter into a spiritual desert. For Kathy, the spiritual desert was a sacred place, a reflective and mysterious place where she could sit with God with her questions and anger and be embraced by God's love. For Matt, the spiritual desert became a place of destruction of his faith and life. His anger turned toward God and anyone who represented God. He understood her illness, and eventual death, as a punishment from God on him personally.

Spiritual deserts are harsh places and crises often complicate an already difficult journey. Spiritual deserts demand honesty, vulnerability, and a willingness to embrace a holy ambiguity. They bring us face-to-face with ourselves and our struggles to depend on God. Spiritual deserts present us with a choice to rely on ourselves and our abilities to navigate life's surprises, or to draw closer to God and embrace the mysterious, which is so often a part of the journey. It is a choice of faith. The spiritual desert calls us to trust God, to follow the pillar of cloud by day and the pillar of fire by night. This is where great faith is exercised and developed.

The Gradual Discovery of Divine Leading

Difficulties in life are not the only way that we find ourselves in spiritual deserts. At times, God leads us into them although this divine leading can often be a gradual experience. In fact, it can be so gradual that we remain unaware of the changing landscapes around us until we stop the business of life long enough to survey the terrain. Unlike crises, which awaken us quickly to our harsh surroundings, God's leading into the desert is less abrupt generally and therefore not so easily recognizable. This gradual movement into the desert, coupled with our general lack of awareness of God's presence in our daily life, accounts for the surprise and confusion we experience as we move further into the desert. The slow transition, however, does allow us to adapt gradually to the transforming environment on a subconscious level. This makes the spiritual awakening a little less of a shock.

The gradual movement into spiritual deserts is easy to perceive in retrospect, but it is difficult to see when it is actually occurring. Just minutes from my home, to the east on Highway 30 and Interstate 84, lies the Columbia River Gorge with its picturesque scenery and legendary waterfalls. The gradual transformation of the landscape as one drives eastward through the gorge is so subtle that it can easily go unnoticed. The terrain near the west end of the gorge is green and lush, filled with Douglas Firs, Big Leaf Maples, Noble Firs, Red Alders, and Western Red Cedars. The ground is covered with ferns and a variety of other plant life. Trees are draped in moss that serves as hosts for sprouting ferns. Due to the amount of rainfall we receive each year, moss grows on everything that does not move. In addition, there are a series of cascading waterfalls fed by streams that flow into small rivers leading back into the grand Columbia. Life is abundant and apparent. However, as the drive continues to the east, ever so slowly, the temperature increases and the deep green hues begin to give way to golden browns as the trees become fewer and the ground more exposed. Unearthed rock formations reveal layers of sediment that reflect the harsh history of the landscape. Lava rocks begin to bulge out of the soil announcing one's arrival in the desert. One begins to wonder what happened to the trees and the greenery of the landscape. Ever so slowly, the landscape changes until it becomes obvious that you have arrived in the desert. Our entry into spiritual deserts can be so gradual that we fail to recognize the transition until it is so obvious that it is unmistakable.

However, the fact that our movement into spiritual deserts may be gradual does not diminish the difficulty of the desert experience. We face many of the same challenges whether we enter the desert through crisis or gradually. The gradual movement into the desert causes us to wrestle with the perplexing reality that God leads us into desert landscapes. This realization is quickly followed by feelings of loss, fear, anger, abandonment, and loneliness. These emotions signal the beginning of a new level of authenticity that is vital to the desert experience. Spiritual deserts provide focus, heighten our awareness of God, open us up to reflection, and prepare us for something we cannot see or hear without the clarity that spiritual deserts can provide.

Spiritual deserts are instruments of God to help us not only to hear, but to listen earnestly to God. God consistently led people into the desert, where they could discover clarity of mind by struggling with God and themselves. The Israelites, Elijah, Jesus, St. Antony, Amma Theodora, and Celtic Christians provide testament to the divine call into the desert. Laura Swan has suggested that the early Desert Mothers and Fathers felt called to physical deserts to refine their inner strength and resolve and deepen their sense of utter dependence on God. The desert was a place of death, a place to die to the false self and false supports and to bury old ways and attitudes.[8] Spiritual desert experiences draw our attention to the falseness of our lives, to the pretense that we too often put on for others. The desert is a place to die and be reborn as a child of the harsh terrain.

There is a strange call that emanates from the desert. The Desert Fathers and Mothers heard it, as did the prophets and Jesus. The desert shaped the Israelites into a nation, teaching them to depend on God. For Elijah, the desert served as a place of rest and nourishment, providing sanctuary for him to reflect and continue the work of God. Jesus struggled in the desert to embrace his ministry and understand himself. The Desert Fathers and Mothers formed communities of prayer and reflection in the desert in order to draw closer to God. These are a few examples of those whom God had led into the desert.

We anguish to articulate the desert experience and often deny the pain of the desert because we cannot imagine God calling us into such a harsh place. And yet, the desert is a place of transformation for those who are far away from God and those who are near. The Spirit of God led Jesus into the desert to struggle with life, ministry, and temptations. It should not be inconceivable that God also leads us into spiritual deserts, not as a punishment, but as a blessing. God desires intimacy with us, an intimacy that flows from grace, an intimacy that calls us to a greater awareness. The desert spiritual landscape facilitates this process.

Whether we enter spiritual deserts through crisis or through divine leading, we discover that deserts reveal our spiritual and theological weaknesses, our attempts to hide from either God, or ourselves and our struggles to trust God. Desert spirituality demands honesty, vulnerability, and humility. It calls us to account for the stewardship of our lives. It does not allow us to play the games we have learned so well from the Church and society, games that would have us continue to live artificial lives while avoiding authenticity. Spiritual deserts strip away the superficial and bring us to a place of clarity and authenticity. Although the desert strips away much of the baggage that we have collected, it also offers us divine grace and the possibility of transforming the harsh landscape into a sacred place. It is only as time elapses that we become reflective enough to receive the divine lessons of desert spirituality.

Lessons From Spiritual Deserts

As we venture through spiritual desert experiences, we begin to discover the rich lessons that the desert has to teach us about ourselves and our relationship with God. Like mountain and valley spirituality, deserts embody wonderful lessons that God intends for us to apply to our journey through all of the spiritual landscapes of life. These lessons can lead us to greater intimacy with God, better knowledge of ourselves, and more loving service to one another.

The lessons of desert spirituality are paradoxical. The desert requires us to *release* our baggage while inviting us to *embrace* God's grace. In addition, it beckons us to live in the sacred tension between *clarity* and *holy ambiguity*. These seemingly contrasting ideas aid us in the development of faith and patience. They heighten our spiritual awareness, and increase our skills of hearing and listening to God. The spiritual desert facilitates clarity of vision, the release of burdens, an embrace of grace, and a willingness to dwell in the ambiguity of God. These are the valuable lessons of desert spirituality. They are the reasons that the desert is a sacred place. Those who would avoid the desert spiritual landscape miss those priceless treasures.

Release and Embrace

As we travel through the desert, there is a point where we begin to take a serious inventory of the accumulated stuff that we carry. Past hurts, wounds, low self-esteem, or anger from unresolved relationships, account for a portion of stuff we carry. The journey through harsh desert terrain confronts us with the realization that we have a lot of accumulated baggage. This baggage stands between us and a greater knowledge and intimacy with God. It is a barrier! We are often slow to release our spiritual baggage, even though it burdens our journey and clouds our vision. The true question of the desert, Belden Lane reminds us, is "How much can I leave behind?"[9] The terrain quickly reminds us that baggage only complicates the journey. A few years ago I commissioned a student to do a series of paintings for the college chapel centered on the theme "Journey Through Life." While each painting depicted a particular landscape of life, I was taken by the image of the desert sojourn. The painting portrayed a person struggling to carry a very large pack through the desert. With a closer look, I discovered that behind the figure lay a trail of items that had been abandoned. These items no longer held value in the harsh desert terrain. They were more trouble than they were worth and therefore were abandoned on the side of the trail. The traveler simply desired to lighten his baggage and make the journey easier; however, the backpack was still filled with many things. Stories of pioneers on the Oregon Trail reflect the hard decisions to leave precious belongings along the trail in order to survive the journey. The wagon-load was often too heavy for muddy trails and mountain passes. My student's painting invited the viewer to contemplate how much more will be left behind. We are left with our imaginations to envision how the desert sojourn unfolded for the person in the painting. At the same time we realize that we too must release our baggage to make it through the desert. This all comes through reevaluating and identifying what is non-essential. Those who began the journey west only brought what they thought was essential for life; however, the rigors of wilderness travel required a reevaluation of those essential items.

The sojourn through the spiritual desert demands that we face the realities of life with honesty. The desert thrusts us toward a process of evaluating our lives. Through honest reflection, we are able to identify and release all that we have discovered to God. This is a crucial part of the spiritual desert experience, and it remains the cause of much of our initial struggle. We want to hold on to what is safe and known, but we are being called to risk and venture into the mysterious. Release requires us to exercise great faith, by which we decide to put down those things that hold us back from a deeper honesty and venture into the unknown, where old paradigms may no longer work. It takes a great deal of vulnerability to release the baggage that we have collected, even when it distracts us from God. Release is a liberating experience and is central to the desert sojourn. We are bound by so much and yet remain unaware of it. In the desert, God penetrates our soul and provokes us to evaluate our entire life, our faith, and the old paradigms on which our faith has been constructed. God stands ready to liberate us from our religiosity, but we are slow to release the dysfunctional areas of our faith. The struggle between our understanding of faith and the faith that God is calling us to lies at the heart of the faith crisis many people experience in spiritual deserts. It is hard to lay down our preconceived religious notions, even when they no longer stimulate our faith and nurture our relationship with God. We are so afraid to give up or even question a faith that we have never really owned, often embracing a formulation of faith that is shallow. We struggle to let go of our control on life and embrace God's grace, but there is something wonderfully liberating about releasing control along with our accumulated religious baggage. The spiritual desert requires us to own and claim a deeper faith.

As a college professor, I have seen students struggle through the harsh realities of spiritual desert experiences. They become confused when their easy answers to difficult questions of life no longer satisfy their curiosity or logic. At the same time they will defend to the death a faith that they have never really owned nor understood. Gently, I have tried to invite them to release their baggage and embrace the grace that God offers to us. Our experiences in the desert allow us to receive and appreciate a grace that is all the richer and more abundant in the desert. For many, release means betrayal of their religious heritage, a rejection of their tradition, and the loss of meaning. It is difficult to perceive, at the time, that the desert sojourn is not a place to lose one's faith, but a place to truly discover it. This discovery occurs through a process of releasing ourselves to God and embracing divine grace in a new way. When babies begin to walk, they hold on to whatever is around them. They only want to let go when they can reach out to another object; however, there are times when the space between objects is so great that they must choose another path or risk walking without the safety of holding on. Embracing the grace of God is like navigating the space between objects. It is the point when we must let go and attempt to walk. Without something solid to hold on to we are afraid. We may fall down. But if we do, God, like a parent, will help us up, hold our hand, and lead us.

Spiritual deserts call us to embrace both the grace of God and the discoveries that we made concerning the world, God, and ourselves while on our sojourn through the desert. Our ability to embrace both grace and our desert discoveries is a result of a growing process stimulated by the spiritual sojourn. We may have heard about the grace of God on numerous occasions; however, the desert teaches us how to walk in grace. Walking in grace is not an easy thing to describe or define, especially to those who have not yet experienced it. Walking in grace requires us to embrace God in our innermost being, to open ourselves up to the movement of the Holy Spirit, and to let go of our need to control. Embracing God's grace so as to walk in grace is like riding a bicycle with your hands stretched outward. Letting go of the handlebars while the wind blows through your hair is a freeing experience. You learned early on how to balance the bicycle and guide it by turning the handlebars. But at some point, you become so comfortable with the bicycle and balance flows so easily that you can ride and guide the bicycle without touching the handlebars. Embracing God's grace on a deeper level is simply a transition from something that you have known to something that you feel and live. For those walking in grace, the desert becomes a sacred place where God is mysterious and Christianity is more than a system of beliefs—it is a way of life. The reflective environment that the desert fosters enables us to learn about our gifts, our weaknesses, our hopes, and ourselves. Parker Palmer suggested, "we arrive in this world with birthright gifts—then we spend the first half of our lives abandoning them or letting others disabuse us of them." He goes on to say, "then—if we are awake, aware, and able to admit our loss—we spend the second half trying to recover and reclaim the gift we once possessed."[10] Spiritual deserts awaken us to our "birthright gifts" and call on us to develop them and exercise them for the glory of God and the betterment of humanity. This discovery is one of the wonderful fruits of the desert experience. While desert spirituality strips away the artificial, it also reveals the hidden and unveils giftedness, which can be lost in the mélange of life and religiosity. Spiritual deserts facilitate a clarity of mind and heart that allows us to release and embrace.

Clarity and Holy Ambiguity

As we release our baggage and begin to embrace God's grace, we begin to discover a heightened awareness of God's presence. We slowly become mindful of the desert as a sacred place where our understanding and perception of God is enhanced. The difference between hearing God and listening to God becomes more distinct as faith, patience, and trust begin to develop in a deeper way. Slowly we arrive at a sense of clarity; yet we are more mindful of the mysterious nature of God.

Spiritual deserts capture our attention, inspire our imaginations, and invite us to release our baggage, embrace grace, and seek a spiritual clarity that has perhaps eluded us in other landscapes. Clarity of mind and heart is a byproduct of releasing the things of life that cloud the face of God. The desert simply facilitates that clarity. As the superficial things fall away, we perceive with freshness our journey with God and indeed life itself. The purging of the desert leaves us naked, transparent, and vulnerable before God. With all that was hidden now revealed, we are left with authenticity, which in turn brings about a certain clarity and a greater awareness of God.

There is no place to flee from God's sight. The presence of God is a constant; yet often we remain unaware of it. Slowly, as we travel the desert sojourn, we begin to realize that God is, in fact, present in all of the spiritual landscapes of our lives. This stimulates a search for God in ways we never conceived of before we walked through the desert. No longer is God limited to mountaintop epiphanies. The desert awakens us to the reality that God is our constant companion.

Clarity of mind and heart, along with the heightened awareness that accompanies it, enables us to hear and to listen to God. Hearing is a physical ability that most of us are born with; however, listening is a skill that can be constantly developed. Adam and Eve heard God moving through the garden in the cool of the evening, but they did not listen. One might suggest that on several occasions biblical characters heard God but did not exercise the patience needed to listen to God and receive clarity of mind and heart. Biblical scholars can debate Abraham's understanding of a call to sacrifice Isaac or Joshua's belief that the Israelites should kill every man, woman, and child in a given city. These are debates best left to biblical scholars; however, we too struggle to develop the patience and skills to listen to God.

Many Christians struggle to discover God's will for their life because they do not know how to listen to and for God. For many, prayer is a one-way experience in which they talk, while expecting God to listen. Sitting in silence and opening ourselves to the movement of the Spirit of God is an unfamiliar means of prayer for many. As a result, when we hear the movement of God through the landscapes of our lives, we immediately react, often without the patience to wait a little longer and listen to what we hear. It is an issue of trust and control. Desert Mothers cultivated a heart engaged in intense listening. As they grew in self-awareness, they achieved a clarity of vision that enabled them to filter the many voices of the world and listen to the voice of God.[11] The conflict between hearing and listening is the willingness to trust before acting. We are not accustomed to hearing God, so when we do, we want to act. However, if we do not listen carefully, we miss the message. Wendy Wright suggested that listening involves a delicate intersection of the human heart and the vast and silent mystery of God.[12] Clarity requires a willingness to trust, a willingness to let go, a willingness to be led, and a willingness to listen.

"The desert is the place where we are forced to live with our questions along with the ambiguities and paradoxes of our life."[13] Desert clarity brings us to a place where we can begin to embrace holy ambiguity and divine mystery. Ambiguity is a difficult concept to embrace, especially for those who like to control everything around them. Many Americans have little room for mystery or unknown elements on their journey. Ambiguity stands in paradoxical tension with clarity. In a strange blending of concepts, desert struggles bring us to a point of sacred clarity. This clarity, however, does not mean that all of life's questions are suddenly answered or that all mysteries are revealed. The desert journey only opens up the doors of our heart and the sashes of our eyes to the sacred. The resulting clarity stimulates our faith and our ability to trust God through the journey of the unknown.

Simeon and Anna clearly believed that one day they would see the chosen one, but they had to rest in holy ambiguity for years before they held the child Jesus (Luke 2:2-40). As graduation approaches, college seniors often come into my office searching for direction. They know God has called them, and they have prepared themselves for ministry; but they are not always clear about what comes next. In fact, sometimes they are frightened and confused. God's call is so clear to them and yet they struggle for details. I encourage them to rest in holy ambiguity as a sacred place where they can experience peace in uncertainty. The desert teaches us a deeper sense of trust and patience, which allows us to rest in the mysteries of God. Embracing divine ambiguity requires a type of faith that spiritual deserts stimulate, a type of faith that requires us to walk without sight, to rest in peace during uncertainty, and to rely on God in new ways. Embracing holy ambiguity allows us to accept the mysterious invitation to walk with God in complete faith. This allows our faith to develop to the point that we can embrace the holy ambiguity that spiritual deserts offer. We can develop patience, an ability to wait for clarity without becoming destructive in our relationship with God or others. Patience allows us to rest in ambiguity as a sacred place, perhaps a place of preparation for the next segment of our journey.

Oasis: Rest and Reflection

The journey through the desert is draining. Even when we are awakening to the rich lessons of the landscape, we still struggle to release, embrace, discover, and respond in the ways that the spiritual sojourn requires. At the time when we believe that we cannot go any further on our desert journey, we often encounter an oasis. The oasis is a blessing from God that allows us to rest, reflect, and prepare ourselves to continue the journey.

This resting place provides water and shade so we can pause and refresh ourselves. Here we can reflect on our journey with God thus far and consider what lies ahead. The oasis allows us a space to process God's revelation, to think about how we are being transformed and to slowly begin to embrace divine mystery. Without oases, the desert journey would be deadly. Even the desert dwellers and caravan leaders utilized oases to survive. They knew where to find the oases as they traveled through the desert trade routes. There, they pitched their tents, rested their herds, ate, drank, and told stories of journeys past and present. Oases, however, are isolated and require pilgrims to reenter the desert in order to continue their journey. Oases can occur at place where we have an opportunity to take a break from the business of life long enough to reflect. For some, it may be at a cabin on the lake or a mountain home or a place at the beach. Or, it may be at a favorite tree that you climbed so often when you were young. Now you find that you are satisfied just to sit in its shade and think. These are vital yet neglected parts of the spiritual desert metaphor. The oasis provides us with an opportunity to rest, catch our breath, gather our thoughts, and reflect on the discoveries we have made during our desert sojourn. It is often in retrospect that we begin to understand the journey and harvest its lessons. We need to take time to slow down and incorporate the blessings. Oases also present us with two cautions. First, an oasis can offer a great temptation to stay. Pilgrims weary of the desert journey can be tempted to stay in the oasis and continue on the journey. The oasis reminds some pilgrims of mountaintop experiences that had been valued so highly. Oases and mountaintops have some commonalities. They are resting places with God that offer safe space to reflect and interact with God. They provide a certain level of assurance and stimulate a divine familiarity that brings blessings. It becomes tempting to return to a pre-desert understanding of God and forget the struggles that we have passed through. It is tempting to pick up the baggage we had released and return to the old paradigms that provided little stimulation for growth. If we give in to this temptation, we have failed to learn the lessons of the spiritual desert, and we will soon find ourselves struggling through the desert once more.

Second, an oasis can be mistaken as an indication that one has completed the spiritual desert experience, when, in fact, it is only a resting place to sit for a while before continuing the desert sojourn. Countless times I have encountered those who have struggled with the desert spiritual experience and mistaken an oasis as a mountaintop. Their struggles have been deep and their pain intense. Students have come into my office and were quick to proclaim their conquest of the spiritual desert. With a newfound energy, which they liken to that of mountaintop spirituality, they embrace the spiritual familiarity that provides some comfort for their struggles. I warn them that their experience may simply be an oasis in the desert and not an indication of the completion of their journey.

A good indication that one is experiencing an oasis and not exiting the desert is a quick reoccurrence of a desert experience. A spiritual high is quickly followed by a disappointing low. The desert has returned. This may be a signal that one has missed the beauty and richness that the desert spiritual sojourn has to offer. It may also mean simply that there are more deserts to cross before journey's end.

The Desert as Sacred Place

Out of all of the spiritual landscapes of life, the desert is perhaps the most difficult terrain to travel, but it also provides some of the richest rewards. We soon discover, as did the apostle Paul, that it is in our weakness that we find strength, and it is through struggle that we mature. This is a timeless lesson of the spiritual desert.

Spiritual deserts change our perspective on life and our ability to understand and respond to God. Deserts call us inward toward honest reflection and downward to dwell in the innermost parts of our being where we sit with God. They are places to mature in our faith, raise hard questions of our journey, and struggle with ourselves.

At some point on our desert sojourn, the desert blooms. It is transformed from a place of death and desolation to an environment filled with life and beauty. This glorious transformation is a result of our changing perception, maturing faith, and authentic struggles. The desert no longer represents a place of separation, but has instead become an intimate environment in which to embrace God.

The spiritual desert is a place of discovery, by which we come to a turning point in our desert experience. Spiritual deserts provide a new way of seeing that allows us to look into the "heart of a thing, to see beyond, to take time, to gaze." It is a "God-given way of seeing, not to

59

possess and to control but to stand back in wonder and gratitude."[14] The desert provides a new type of sight. David Adam summarized the heart of spiritual desert experiences well:

> The Desert of God may be a place of renunciation but it is also where the senses are heightened rather than dulled, where life is not settled but being forever extended. The call of the desert is a call to see beyond the obvious, to reach out for the invisible and to put our trust in our God. The desert is not a hiding place but a place where all is revealed. If the desert is a place of pruning, it is a pruning that life may blossom and grow in the right direction. It is not so much a return to the natural as to the supernatural, to discover the extra-ordinary that is ever-present in the ordinary.[15]

The desert provides us with a unique perspective that invites us to view ourselves, our world, and God in authentic and fresh ways. As a result, spiritual deserts prepare us to dwell mindfully with God as we become more comfortable in the presence of God. The spiritual desert is a harsh landscape that has much to teach us. As we add the lessons of deserts to those of mountains and valleys, we are better prepared to grow and mature in our relationship with God in all the landscapes of life.

Endnotes

1. Belden Lane, *The Solace of Fierce Landscapes: Exploring Desert and Mountain Spirituality* (New York: Oxford University Press, 1998), 195.
2. Thomas Keating, *Invitation to Love: The Way of Christian Contemplation* (New York: Continuum, 1994), 77.
3. Esther de Waal, *The Celtic Way of Prayer: The Recovery of the Religious Imagination* (New York: Doubleday, 1997), 1.
4. Laura Swan, *The Forgotten Desert Mothers: Sayings, Lives and Stories of Early Christian Women* (New York: Paulist, 2001), 15.
5. Walter Brueggemann, *The Spirituality of the Psalms,* Facets (Minneapolis: Fortress, 2002). See chapter 3 for a detailed explorations of this concept.
6. Quoted from Laura Swan, *The Forgotten Desert Mothers: Saying, Lives and Stories of Early Christian Women* (New York: Paulist, 2001), 43.
7. Keating, *Invitation to Love,* 84.
8. Swan, *The Forgotten Desert Mothers,* 15.
9. Lane, *The Solace of Fierce Landscapes,* 167.

10. Parker Palmer, *Let Your Life Speak: Listening for the Voice of Vocation* (San Francisco: Jossey-Bass, 2000), 12.

11. Swan, *The Forgotten Desert Mothers,* 31.

12. Wendy M. Wright, "Desert Listening," *Weavings* 9.3 (1994) 10.

13. Swan, *The Forgotten Desert Mothers,* 168.

14. Esther de Waal "Attentiveness," *Weavings* 27.4 (2002) 23.

15. David Adam, *A Desert in the Ocean* (New York: Paulist, 2000), 4.

5
The Ordinary as Sacred Place
Valley Dwelling

Valleys are the places where we live, work, and play. We spend most of our lives as valley dwellers, living on the plains, at the foot of mountains, and in the low places that are fertile and abundant with life. Spiritual valleys are under-recognized and underappreciated metaphors in the Christian spiritual landscape; however, they are the primary terrains of our lives. Generally, valleys do not reveal anything extraordinary, only the common beauty of the familiar things of life that we slowly grow to ignore. However, if we pause long enough, we may see that the ordinary is filled with the sacred. We may perceive God's presence blossoming in the valley. If we restrict our awareness of God to the extraordinary, then we miss the expressions of God in the simplest things: a smiling baby, a blooming flower, or a sunset. As our spiritual awareness increases, however, we are able to recognize God's movements in spiritual valleys both in the ordinary and extraordinary.

Valleys call us to pay attention to the ordinary and to be mindful of God's presence in our daily experiences; however, to perceive the expressions of God in the ordinary requires intentionality. Francis de Sales, a late sixteenth-century priest, suggested two principles that can assist us in being more mindful of God's presence. First, we must realize that God's presence is in all things and all places. No place or thing in this world is without the divine presence. De Sales suggested, "Everyone knows this truth but everyone does not try to bring it home."[1] Second, God not only is present in the world around us, but God is also present in a most particular manner in our hearts and in the very center of our spirits.[2] Originally, de Sales' comments were directed toward a Christian audience; however, it is important to contemplate how God is present in all of creation and how Christians understand the divine presence in the world. Spiritual valleys facilitate a greater awareness of God's presence around us and within us. Thomas Merton believed that every moment and every event in our life plant spiritual seeds. These seeds are God's continual attempt to speak to us; however, most of the innumerable seeds perish and are lost because we are unaware of them or unprepared to receive them and respond.[3] Merton invites us to experience life as a sacrament, as an expression of God's grace.

Valley spirituality invites pilgrims to dwell mindfully with God and embrace the reality of God's indwelling presence. The lessons of awareness and reflection derived from valleys empower us to see God, not just in the common, simple, and ordinary experiences of life, but also in the deserts and on the mountains. From a valley perspective, all landscapes offer us insight into the sacred and foster a deeper relationship with God. The valley serves as a balance between the spiritual highs of mountaintop encounters and the struggles so common to spiritual deserts. Valleys allow us space to reflect on the lessons we have learned from our mountain and desert sojourns while at the same time inspiring us to embrace the dynamics of everyday life as sacred expressions of God.

The purpose of this chapter is to invite pilgrims to recognize the sacred in the ordinary by exploring the beauty and dynamics of valley spirituality. Spiritual valleys are places where we learn to become comfortable with God and the reality of God's indwelling presence. By calling attention to some key elements of valley spirituality, we can gain access to some of the common spiritual experiences and frustrations that we face on our journeys with God, and we can find a language to describe them meaningfully, both to ourselves and to others.

Spiritual valleys are often misunderstood as transitional places on the way to other landscapes. This attitude allows us to dismiss any real appreciation for the valley landscape and the priceless lessons that it has to teach us. We need to reevaluate the valley as both the primary landscape of our life and a sacred place in which God is revealed in the ordinary. Key elements of valley spirituality highlight awareness and reflection as vehicles to open us to the ordinary as sacred space. By increasing our awareness of God in the world, taking time for spiritual reflection, and realizing that we need not go elsewhere to encounter God, we start to embrace the valley as our spiritual home and begin to internalize the reality that God dwells within us. This "incarnational reality" is the fruit of the spiritual valley. It enables us to dwell mindfully with God and to be aware of our responsibilities for God living in and through us.

The Valley and Incarnational Reality

Incarnational Reality is the cornerstone of valley spirituality. Embracing God's indwelling presence heightens our awareness of the divine and enables us to envision God as a constant companion on our journey. Our capacity to be valley dwellers and visualize the ordinary as sacred place is greatly determined by our awareness of God. If we embody the reality that God is dwelling within us through the power of the Holy Spirit, then we are inclined to see God actively engaged in the ordinary, where God becomes a reality of life, a familiar presence, and a constant companion. We come to see the world as a sacrament; the mind becomes the playground for God; and spiritual landscapes of life serve as the stages on which we live out our journey. Embracing an incarnational reality enables us to envision spiritual valleys as dynamic places where God is ever present in the simplest, most common and ordinary things of life. It redirects our attention from searching out spiritual highs to the realization that God is present here and now regardless of our current spiritual landscape.

Biblically and historically, the incarnation refers to God becoming human in the person of Jesus. In Jesus, God was revealed and expressed to humanity in a unique way. God took on human form and dwelt among us for about thirty-three years. Jesus was and continues to be the ultimate incarnation of God, intimately connected to God in a mysterious way that we still do not completely understand. Scripture clearly expresses the mysterious bond between God and Jesus. God was in Christ reconciling the world (2 Corinthians 5:19). The Word was made flesh and dwelt among us (John 1:14). "I and the Father are one" (John 10:30). These words of Jesus and others emphasize the intimate connection and mysterious relationship between God and Jesus. The scripture even utilized the image of father and son to denote the closeness of the relationship. Jesus lived a life that embodied God. He reflected God in his teachings, general demeanor, and responses to others. People were amazed at his teachings, transformed by his touch, and challenged by his integrity.

Jesus led people to a greater understanding of God. He prayed, "I have revealed you to those whom you gave me out of the world. They were yours; you gave them to me and they have obeyed your word. Now they know that everything you have given me comes from you. For I gave them the words you gave me and they accepted them. They knew with certainty that I came from you, and they believed that you sent me" (John 17:6-9). Jesus was and remains a conduit for God, making God accessible to humanity, but what are the implications of an ongoing incarnation?

The Call and Responsibility of Incarnational Reality

Accepting the incarnation as an ongoing process is not universally acknowledged, and yet it is biblical and historically rooted. Ronald Rolheiser declared, "The incarnation is still going on and it is just as real and as radically physical as when Jesus of Nazareth, in the flesh, walked the dirt roads of Palestine."[4] Through Jesus Christ, God is ever present in us! This is the "incarnational reality." It is simply the realization that God dwells in us at the essence of our being. Embracing an incarnational reality allows us to undertake a fresh understanding of God's intention to be in an intimate relationship with us. We are created in the image and likeness of God. Through sin we have lost our closeness to God along with our awareness of God's constant presence; however, through Jesus we have received forgiveness, allowing God to be birthed in us, growing and developing within our hearts, minds, and, perhaps most importantly, our imaginations in order that we may express divine love, mercy, grace, and peace to the world around us, just as Jesus did. Paul used the phrase "putting on Christ." Thomas à Kempis referred to it as the imitation of Christ. John Wesley referred to an incarnational reality as growing in grace. By whatever name, the concept is the same, "Be Like Jesus!" We are not Jesus Christ, and I am not attempting to claim that Christians are in some way cosmic redeemers; however, I am suggesting that we are more than we think we are. Dwelling in the valley with God allows us opportunities to reflect and live out God's presence in the world. Our true identity lies in the reality that we are children of God, the beloved sons and daughters of God. Jesus revealed this truth to us.[5] Paul called us to put on Christ, and accept the responsibility of being little Christ to the world, the aroma of Christ to God, the fragrance of life and death (2 Corinthians 2:14-16). Jesus said, "You are the salt of the earth." "You are the light of the world" (Matthew 5:13a and 14a). He did not say *some* day we will be salt and light, but instead declares that we are already expressions of God to the world. We are the "Children of God," and the "Body of Christ." These biblical images reinforce our deep incarnational connection to God. The incarnation was not just a thirty-year experiment focused in Jesus, or a one-time incursion by God into human history. It is an ongoing reality for those who choose to invite God to fill their lives.[6] This, taken seriously, transforms our spiritual journey and changes our perception of the spiritual landscapes of our lives. Incarnational reality calls us to a greater responsibility in our journey with God and in our treatment of others. It invites us into an everyday mysticism while calling us to live out the social implications of salvation. This is why incarnational reality fits so beautifully in spiritual valleys. It necessitates that we live a Christ-like life in our everyday, normal experiences. While it is empowering on one level to be mindful of God's indwelling presence, it is terrifying on another. Major responsibilities accompany living out the incarnation in spiritual valleys. Scripture is filled with incarnational images and metaphors that perplex and yet intrigue our imagination. The responsibilities of being disciples of Christ reach to the deepest realms of our essence. During a final post-resurrection visit to his disciples, Jesus breathed on them and said: "Receive the Holy Spirit. If you forgive the sins of any, they are forgiven them; if you retain the sins of any, they are retained" (John 20:23). In another context, Jesus responded to Peter's confession at Caesarea Philippi that Jesus was the Christ, the living Son of God, by saying, "I will give you the keys to the kingdom of heaven, and whatever you bind on earth will be bound in heaven, and whatever you loose on earth will be loosed in heaven" (Matthew 16:19). These two passages call us to the deepest levels of the embodiment of Jesus. They forward great responsibilities to those who would dare to put on Christ and live out the reality that we are incarnational reflections of God. Spiritual valleys provide stable and safe environments for us to live out incarnational realities.

Spiritual Valleys

Spiritual valleys are the dominant landscape of our lives, landscapes filled with God's presence expressed in the ordinary things of life; however, it remains a difficult task for many Christians to embrace the valley as their spiritual home. A popular focus toward mountaintop spiritual encounters has led many Christians to ignore the sacred in the ordinary, running the risk of missing God's movements around us. While mountaintop experiences are important and hold treasures for our journey, we do not live on mountaintops. We live in valleys where we spend the majority of our spiritual lives. Recognizing the sacred in the ordinary requires awareness, attentiveness, and assistance from others. Our ability to be sensitive to God's activity in life and our willingness to pause long enough to appreciate the sacred in the ordinary are keys to opening ourselves to an entirely new dynamic in our relationship with God. Awareness and reflection are two treasures of spiritual valleys. They prepare us to embrace the reality of God's indwelling presence and view creation from a fresh perspective. The beauty of God is abundant in the ordinary things of the valley; however, we can lose sight of divine expressions in the ordinary if we only focus on the dramatic and spectacular. Much like the Old Testament prophet Elijah, we look for God in the extraordinary, the mighty wind, the shaking earth, and the consuming fire. Yet much to our surprise, God often does not speak in the extraordinary ways, but in the still whispers that require attentiveness, listening, heightened awareness, and reflection (1 Kings 19:11-18). Ironically, we search for a God who is already standing beside us, attempting to reveal the sacred in our present surroundings. Yet we remain unaware, continuing to limit our search for God to mountaintops and dynamic spiritual experiences. God is right here, right now in the simplest things of life. We just need a little help to see the world through the eyes of Jesus and to be sensitive to the movements of God. If we are willing, we can see the world as a sanctuary and life as a sacrament.

Lessons from the Valley: Awareness & Reflection

Spiritual awareness and reflection are vital components of valley spirituality. Awareness requires intentionality and a desire to be attentive to life as we open ourselves to various expressions of God. Once we become more mindful of God's presence, we are drawn to reflect, to ponder, and to process our experience. Awareness and reflection, however, are not restricted to the landscape of the valley. They are important aspects of desert spirituality, where the harsh environment demands our attention and awareness, but also provides opportunities for us to reflect and rest before completing our desert sojourn. Mountain spirituality also has components of awareness and reflection. Our awareness is heightened on mountaintops in a different fashion than in the desert or the valleys; nonetheless, we experience a greater awareness of God's presence, which leads to spiritual reflection. The reason for highlighting awareness and reflection as a part of valley spirituality is to place these two key elements for our spiritual journey within the realm of normal, common, and everyday aspects of life. Mountain and desert landscapes tend to emphasize awareness and reflection in extreme environments. As a result, pilgrims can easily overlook their importance to spiritual valleys. However, it is precisely because the valley invites us to awareness and reflection in the ordinary that we explore the valley in this chapter.

Awareness: Seeing the Ordinary as Sacred

Painters, poets, musicians, and occasionally theologians help us to see the familiar and ordinary in extraordinary ways. They increase our awareness and open doors to the sacred by highlighting the common things of life and inviting us to reflect on their beauty. They provide access to something that is already in us, searching for words and images to be expressed. A great poem, a beautiful ballet, or an intriguing painting can invite us to a greater awareness of beauty in life and point us to the spiritual. Madeleine L'Engle has suggested that all true art is religious at its essence.[7] The arts have a way of tapping into our spirits, revealing truth and beauty while

68

inviting us to sit and reflect. No magic formula can increase one's spiritual awareness. The simplest way to begin seeing God actively at work in the world is just to look. Nature, art, music, literature, and Scripture reveal God in particular ways. We are invited to seek and be assured that we will find God when we seek with all of our heart (Jeremiah 29:13). Jesus said, "Seek and you shall find, knock and the door will be open" (Matthew 7:7). As we begin to seek God, we may be surprised where we see God manifested. There is a "God-given way of seeing," according to Esther de Waal. This way of seeing does not possess or control, but stands back in wonder and gratitude.[8] As our search for God leads to discovery, our increased awareness continues to open our eyes to the sacred in the ordinary—not just in art and music, but also in nature and in other people. The entire world becomes a playground for the divine and an opportunity for humans to encounter God.

Sometimes we need a little help to do something as simple as look for God. I often begin spiritual retreats by inviting people especially to look for God during the weekend and to be mindful of the ways God is expressed to them over the course of the retreat. At the close of our time together, we take time to articulate the various ways we have encountered God. People often surprise themselves as they recall the numerous experiences in which they were especially aware of God's presence in the span of a few days. The rhythm of the ocean, the setting of the sun, a conversation with a friend, the music sung around a campfire, and the still small voice speaking into their hearts and minds all serve as testimonies of their awareness of God's presence and their spiritual growth. Once we begin really looking for God, we discover that God is ever present. Thomas Merton wonderfully expressed the reality of God's presence in the world,

> Life is this simple
> We are living in a world that is absolutely transparent
> and God is shining through it all the time.
> This is not just a fable or a nice story.
> It is true.
> If we abandon ourselves to God
> and forget ourselves,
> we see it sometimes
> and we see it maybe frequently.

God shows Godself everywhere,
in everything,
in people and in things and in nature and in events.
It becomes very obvious that God is everywhere and
in everything and we cannot be without God.
It is impossible.
The only thing is that we don't see it.[9]

It takes time, intentionality, and a pure heart to see God. As our awareness develops, we discover that God is everywhere, in people, things, nature, and events. This is not an attempt at some form of pantheism, only an affirmation of the biblical witness of the Psalmists who were able to hold in tension the transcendence and immanence of God. We begin to realize that we need not go to the mountaintop to experience God. The valley blossoms with God's presence, expressing the sacred in the ordinary. Jesus called attention to spiritual valleys by using the ordinary to communicate the sacred. In fact, through the incarnation, the ordinary is no longer at all what it appears. "Common things, common actions, common relationships are all granted new definition because the holy has once and for all become ordinary in Jesus Christ."[10] He spoke of vineyards and landowners, bread and water, wayward children and homecomings. He took the simplest things of life and invited others to see God in and through the ordinary. Jesus applied a clump of mud to the eyes of a blind man who, upon washing the mud away, gained his sight. At the same time Jesus invited the spiritually blind to open their eyes and see God (John 9:1-41). He used fish and loaves of bread to teach us about God's provisions and compassion for humanity.

Jesus transformed people, increased their spiritual awareness, and revealed God in fresh new ways. Sometimes he utilized the extraordinary, but often he revealed God in the ordinary things of life, enabling humans to envision walking with God as a normal part of life.

The ordinary is overflowing with the sacred every day. I was recently reminded of this while waiting for my wife to finish an appointment at a hair salon. A mother with a newborn baby approached the counter to pay the clerk. She sat the baby, who was in a baby's car seat, on the floor next to her while she settled her account. Like many people, I am fascinated with babies. I found myself focused on the sleeping newborn. Sleeping children look so peaceful and blessed. As I stared at the baby, I noticed that she began to smile, and at points even seemed to laugh. As the mother continued her conversation with the clerk, the sleeping baby continued to smile off and on, as if she was in a pleasant conversation with someone. What would cause a sleeping newborn to smile? What did she see? What do newborn babies dream about, given their limited experiences outside the womb? While I am not sure we can ever answer these questions, we can choose to see God expressed in the smiles of newborn babies. My experience lasted only five or six minutes, but it captured my attention and imagination for the entire day. I do not know what she was smiling about, but it stimulated my imagination. Perhaps children are able to see God in ways we have forgotten. I was blessed to experience a deep sense of God's love and presence through the smile of a baby. It is not difficult to see the extraordinary in the common things of life. It comes with practice as our awareness of God grows. Slowly but surely, we begin to see God more and more in life around us. It is a wonderful thing to see God in the extraordinary; however, we must be careful not to disregard the sacred expressions in the ordinary and daily routines of life.

Sometimes we may be surprised at the places where we experience a greater awareness of God. There are some places we generally assume to be sacred places, such as those set aside for worship, prayer, and the gathering of believers. We expect, for example, to experience God in churches through the reading of Scripture, singing of songs, preaching of the Word, and fellowship with others. However, even in the common acts of worship, we may experience God in unexpected ways. Perhaps it is in others, in simple acts of kindness, or in children that we unexpectedly encounter God. I experienced the extraordinary in the ordinary during a worship experience at the cloister in Andech, Germany. The fifteenth-century cloister is still alive with activity, providing the community with a gathering place for Mass each Sunday morning. I had planned for months to visit the cloister, and I hoped to have time to reflect and sit with God in the chapel. I was blessed to arrive at the monastery on a Sunday morning in time for worship. The small church filled with townspeople, visitors, and tourists. I anticipated the beauty of the church, the sounds of the organ, and the spirit of worship among fellow Christians. My awareness was heightened, my desire to experience God in worship primed, and my imagination was in high gear as I sat and thought about those who had passed through the cloister over the last five hundred years. Grabbing a service book, I took my seat in a pew toward the back just as the service was beginning. My German is poor, but I was able to follow the service, sing the hymns, and say the prayers as my eyes continually gazed around the building. In the pew behind me was a young mother with two children, a girl about four years old and a boy around eighteen months. As the service began, I noticed that the little girl had taken up residence in an old confessional booth off to the side. She was sitting on the piece of wood where thousands had kneeled over the centuries to confess their sins and ask for absolution. She had no awareness of the history of the confessional or imagination about those who had kneeled where she was seated. In playfulness, she had no awareness of sin or the purpose for her confessional seat. She simply made herself comfortable in the confessional and at home in the house of God. Soon, her little brother joined her in this sacred spot, sitting on her lap and drinking from his bottle. All my anticipation of a special encounter with God in the cloister at Andech was realized not just in the beauty of liturgy or the building, but in the simplest expression of the innocence of two small children. The freedom of heart and mind allowed them to be completely comfortable, even playful, in the presence of God. Unfortunately, as we grow older, we tend to lose our innocent view of the world and our playfulness with God.

Valleys are filled with manifestations of God in common and ordinary things of life. We need only to look for them. God invites us to be valley dwellers—to build our homes, live our lives, develop relationships, use our gifts wisely, and walk mindfully with God. Valleys present us with opportunities to increase our awareness of God and to put into practice the lessons we have learned from our mountaintop encounters and desert sojourns.

Reflection: Listening for God

Spiritual reflection is a blessing that naturally flows from a greater awareness of God. It results from our openness to the movement of the Holy Spirit and a sensitivity to the interaction between God and humanity. We sit and think about an image or an experience. We ponder its meaning and work hopefully to discern its purpose. As we let it direct us, we find ourselves even more open and able to listen to the Spirit of God.

Mary, the mother of Jesus, provided a wonderful model of spiritual reflection. She was a master of pondering. Her dynamic experiences with God and the events surrounding the birth and childhood of Jesus provided many occasions that required spiritual reflection. Mary pondered and treasured things in her heart, from her initial encounter with the angel Gabriel (Luke 1:26-38), to the words of the shepherds on the night Jesus was born (Luke 2:8-20), and the testimonies of Simeon and Anna, who met the infant Jesus in the temple (Luke 2: 21-40). She also reflected on the words of the twelve-year-old Jesus as he taught with wisdom in the temple (Luke 2:41-52). She had much on which to reflect, raising questions of meaning, purpose, identity, and direction, both for herself and for Jesus. Is it possible that Mary knew who Jesus was before he did? What a load to carry! Mary's great awareness of God, however, allowed her to open her heart and mind to listen to God and to struggle with what she saw and heard. She mastered spiritual reflection and perhaps even helped Jesus master his skills of reflection. Spiritual reflection flows naturally from experiences like Mary's, but not all experiences convey the presence of God so clearly. Often, it is only in retrospect, through a process of reflection, that we realize we have had a divine encounter. The Old Testament character Jacob was traveling from Beersheba to Haran as the sun began to set (Genesis 28:10-17). He stopped for the night and, taking a stone for a pillow, began to dream of a ladder with angels ascending and descending; and the Lord stood beside him and spoke with him. When he awoke Jacob said, "Surely the Lord is in this place and I did not know it!" (Genesis 28:16). The disciples on the road to Emmaus were unaware that the stranger walking with them was in fact Jesus. It was in the ordinary act of breaking bread that their eyes were opened. They had been talking among themselves about the surreal experiences of the Passion Week. It was only after a long conversation and the departure of Jesus that the disciples realized they had indeed been walking in the presence of Christ. "Were not our hearts burning within us while he was talking to us on the road, while he was opening the scripture to us?" (Luke 21:13-35). God cries out to us every day in thousands of ways; we need only to pause long enough to open ourselves to see and hear. Through ordinary or extraordinary experiences, the valley is filled with occasions for spiritual reflection; however, spiritual reflection is generally a lost art in

American culture. Americans tend to be active rather than contemplative, doers rather than deliberators.[11] Many Christians struggle to sit and pray for three or four minutes without being distracted. As a result, we tend to react before we think through situations. We need to regain the art of spiritual reflection, opening ourselves and allowing the Spirit to lead our thinking and inspire our thoughts. While spiritual reflection cannot be packaged in an instant formula nor designated to an occasional five minute devotional, it must be a regular part of our lives. Spiritual valleys provide safe spaces for us to discover God in fresh ways and explore our developing relationships. Valleys offer us the ordinary as constant reminders of God's closeness. Awareness and reflection are vehicles that empower the transformation of the ordinary and the common into extraordinary encounters with God. The smiling newborn baby and the little girl in the old confessional are simply ordinary occurrences that may have been meaningless to others who observed them. To a heart and mind seeking to be aware of God's presence in the world around us, almost anything can be an occasion for spiritual reflection, a teaching moment for the Holy Spirit, an opportunity to allow a mind to be a playground for God.

Becoming Valley Dwellers

Spiritual valleys highlight the presence of God, the closeness of the divine presence, inviting us to be at home in the presence of God and to see life through the eyes of Jesus. Spiritual valleys provide an environment in which to become more comfortable with God. They allow us to continue to develop the familiarity and intimacy that we discovered while on the mountaintop. Spiritual valleys invite us to re-envision the spiritual journey not as a series of ups and downs, going to and from mountaintops, but as pilgrimages through the various landscapes of life with God as our companion. Awareness and reflection allow us to redirect our attention from a search for God somewhere out beyond the world to the realization that God is present right here, right now. Henri Nouwen said, "To live in the present, we must believe deeply that what is most important is the here and now. We are constantly distracted by things that have happened in the past or that might happen in the future. It is not easy to remain focused on the present."[12] Valley spirituality invites us to dwell and value the present through embracing the ordinary as a reflection of the sacred.

Seeing the ordinary as sacred and learning to make our home in spiritual valleys is a process. It does not happen overnight. In many ways, valley dwelling requires us to set aside some of our religious thinking and refocus our spiritual journey. Valley spirituality redirects our Christian sojourn from questing for mountaintop experiences to accepting the reality that God is ever present around us. Valleys encourage us to walk in the grace of God daily and to embrace the life that grows from such a walk. When we accept the valley as our spiritual home, we realize that every day provides its own opportunity to live thoughtfully with God. Becoming a valley dweller means that we are learning to rest, work, and play in the presence of God. The simplest things in life become occasions to experience divine grace as the ordinary reveals the sacred.

The Valley and Community

Valleys are community places where people dwell together. Unlike desert and mountain sojourns, which tend to be more individually focused, spiritual valleys are communal by nature. Faith communities can experience spiritual deserts and mountains, just as individuals do; however, we seem slow to frame our conversation equally around struggles and celebrations of congregational sojourns. Spiritual valleys give us an opportunity to unpack our individual sojourns through life's various landscapes in the safety and support of faith communities. Valleys provide a communal environment from which to see God in the ordinary things of life, including expressions of God in others. Nouwen suggested, "The closer we come to God, the closer we come to all our brothers and sisters in the human family. . . . God who has chosen us as a dwelling place gives us the eyes to see the God who dwells in others."[13] The communal nature of spiritual valleys provides us space to live out the life of Christ among "those who are being saved and those who are perishing" (2 Corinthians 2:15). The valley brings us one step closer to embracing the reality that God is dwelling in us and in others. However, there are barriers in spiritual valleys that divert our attention from our journey with God and lure us back into a complacency that is so familiar to the valley.

Barriers to Dwelling in Spiritual Valleys

As has been suggested, spiritual valleys invite us to see extraordinary expressions of God in the ordinary things of life. They provide safe spaces to develop awareness and reflection. Barriers, however, can preclude us from embracing valleys and perceiving the sacred in the ordinary. As much as awareness and reflection open us to God, our fast-paced culture and our tendencies to focus on the arrival while ignoring the journey can lead to complacency and cloud our understanding and vision of God. Before we can hope to embrace the spiritual valley and mindfully dwell in the presence of God, we must first overcome the general numbness that slowly consumes us and dulls our senses. Various forms of information and images from television, radio, the internet, billboards, and junk mail bombard us every day. As a result, we are more inclined to ignore our surroundings than to be aware of them. This is one reason advertisers continue to create new ways to get our attention and make us aware of their products. Las Vegas is a city that has mastered getting our attention with flashing signs, neon lights, and a surreal atmosphere. With so many social barriers, it is increasingly difficult to arouse spiritual awareness and compete with a growing need for extreme experiences.

Fast-Paced Society

Our fast-paced world does not provide many opportunities to reflect and be attentive to the movements of God in society. Spiritual awareness and reflection compete with a self-serving society captivated with materialism and empowered by technology. Technology has enabled us to explore new dimensions of reality, develop global communications, gather mind-stretching amounts of information, and move at an ever-increasing pace. While technology has gifted us with more time, we have not always been wise stewards of the time we have saved. Empty spaces are simply filled with other tasks, the acquisition of stuff, longer work hours, or numerous other activities that do not necessarily enhance our relationship with God or others. The American desire for "stuff" often consumes us and captures

76

our imaginations. We dream of bigger homes, nicer cars, or the latest home technology, which can simply mask our need for greater purpose, meaning, and identity. We spend most of our lives in the beauty of spiritual valleys where the ordinary reveals the sacred, and yet we remain unaware as we go about at a faster and faster pace. In the 1950s, President Eisenhower encouraged the construction of interstate highways so Americans could travel around the country more easily and quickly. The increasing number of automobiles burdened the existing road system, which was designed for slower traffic, fewer cars, and farm equipment. Interstate highways provided a more direct route from one point to another, allowing for multiple lanes to travel in the same direction at higher speeds. The "Red Roads," so called because of their color designation on maps, took more travel time because they went through small towns and around farmers' land, and they were designed for only two lanes of traffic. They were not time efficient for those wanting to get somewhere quickly. Interstate highways allowed us to get from one point to another as quickly as possible along the most direct route. Though the interstate system enhances time efficiency, it often requires us to sacrifice beauty for speed.

Interstate 84 runs from Portland, Oregon, eastward through the state. The highway winds along the Columbia River through the beautiful Columbia River Gorge. Countless travelers going east and west on I-84 have glanced at Multnomah Falls, a beautiful 200-foot waterfall, as they have passed. From the interstate one can see the wonderful river, numerous trees, rock formations, and even a few waterfalls. However, if one really wants to see the beauty of the gorge, it is necessary to get off the Interstate, reduce the traveler's speed from 70 mph to 35 mph, and travel the old Columbia River Highway, a two-lane road that winds around the rock formations and through a cathedral-like shaded cover, rich in ferns and moss-covered trees. The old highway reveals a series of waterfalls not visible from the interstate. The sights, sounds, and smells invite travelers to relax and enjoy the beauty of nature. Trails allow folk to walk deeper into the forest revealing even more wonders. Some of the beauty of the gorge can be experienced by traveling 70 mph on Interstate 84, but by getting off the main highway and perhaps even out of the car, one will receive an entirely different experience. Most of us are interstate people who go through life at 70 mph, experiencing some of the beauty of the valley, but generally never taking the time to truly embrace the sacred in the ordinary or reflect on God's expressions in creation. We simply do not take time to slow down, smell the roses, or be aware of our surroundings—time to reflect on life. For too many Christians, awareness of God is limited to a few hours on a designated day of the week. Yet, we struggle and complain that our spiritual lives are empty and our search of divine guidance is often fruitless. Relationships, spiritual and otherwise, require time, effort, and intentionality. I am not suggesting that we should divorce ourselves of technology for the purpose of spiritual enlightenment nor that we return to the "good old days" before interstate highways and fast travel. I am only suggesting that if we desire a fuller relationship with God, then we must take time to be aware of God's presence in the ordinary and allow space for reflection on our experiences.

Arrival and Journey

A second barrier to recognizing and embracing spiritual valleys is closely connected to the first. The fast pace with which our culture functions generates a focus on arrival, the accomplishment of goals, and reaching a certain point, while ignoring or overlooking the value of the journey. A creative tension exists between journey and arrival in the Christian experience. The journey teaches us priceless lessons that prepare us for celebrating arrivals. Arriving at a place after a long journey allows us to rest, reflect, and contemplate the next steps of our sojourn. However, the concept of spiritual arrival is a dominant theological theme in many segments of Christianity that place the focus on heaven and spiritual mountaintops. Now, as Paul says, our citizenship is in heaven, to be sure; but if we focus solely on some eternal reward, we may tend to ignore the needs of others, miss the sacred in the ordinary, and fail to embrace the richness of the spiritual journey. Not only do we often fail to perceive God's presence, but we also miss the purpose of traveling with God through life. These two important elements, journey and arrival, become barriers when we lose the balance between the two. If we focus only on the journey, we may lose sight of the purpose for our journey and burn out or become misguided. On the other hand, if we are fixated with arriving at a point or goal, we are in danger of overlooking the beauty of the journey and the rich lessons that enable us to grow, develop, and continue traveling. The tension between journey and arrival is played out in a variety of ways every day, often without our being aware of it. I experienced this tension with my ten-year-old son on a trip to Paris recently. This was Grant's first time in Paris, so I decided that we would explore the things he wanted to do. Before leaving for France, we had spoken about a few sites that he wanted to see. So each morning, while in Paris, we got up and explored the places he desired. I purchased a pass that allowed us to visit several major sites in the city. After visiting the Eiffel Tower, climbing the bell towers of Notre Dame, riding bicycles around the gardens of Versailles, and having numerous other adventures, I was excited to introduce my son to the treasures of the Louvre. As our time in Paris was drawing to a close, I asked him if there was anything else he wanted to see in Paris. The only thing left on his list was the Mona Lisa, which was located in the Louvre. Unfortunately, after other activities of the day, we arrived about forty-five minutes before closing; but I was still hoping to be able to explain some of the Renaissance masterpieces in the Denon wing of the Louvre. We entered the museum, picked up our map, and proceeded to follow the signs toward the Mona Lisa. As we passed works of Leonardo da Vinci, Titian, Raphael, and the Neoclassical works of David, I attempted to pause and appreciate the beauty of these works, while inviting my son to embrace the awe of the moment. However, his goal was to see the Mona Lisa.

He did not care about all of the other paintings or sculptures. He was on a mission to see the Mona Lisa. We must have made the record for the quickest trip through the Louvre in its entire history. We walked straight to the Mona Lisa, passing world-famous works of art. It took about fifteen minutes to arrive at the Mona Lisa. We paused in front of the painting for a moment to analyze da Vinci's work. Grant turned to me and said, "It's smaller than I thought it would be. Can we go now? I want to get a tee shirt of the Mona Lisa in the gift shop." As it turned out, we spent more time in the gift shop than we did viewing any of the works in the museum.

Our spiritual journey can get so focused on arriving at a spiritual mountaintop that we ignore the beauty of the journey; however, it is the journey that prepares us for the arrival. To understand the Mona Lisa, one needs to experience other paintings in order to have a reference for da Vinci's work. The journey through the Louvre exposes guests to a variety of artists from various periods. Seeing the other paintings opens the way to a greater appreciation of the style and quality of the Mona Lisa. The journey prepares one for the arrival.

The Christian life is a journey with God through the various spiritual landscapes of life with a series of arrivals. In the desert sojourn, an oasis provides a point of arrival, a place of rest and reflection before continuing on the journey. Mountaintops are points of arrival, places of spiritual enrichment and blessing on our journey. However, arrival points do not mark the end of a journey, only a transition from one phase to another. Journey and arrival are dynamic aspects of spiritual life. They become barriers to valley dwelling when the tension between the two is lost.

Complacency

An additional barrier to valley dwelling is complacency. Even if we overcome the other barriers and begin to embrace spiritual valleys, complacency can overtake us slowly. Complacency grows from reaching a level of satisfaction and choosing to rest at a place of arrival. Slowly and without fanfare, we slip into a routine that can lead to losing sight of the bigger journey. It is the same temptation that we face in the desert oases and mountaintop moments. Once we discover a restful place in which to dwell safely, we can quickly forget that life is a journey with God through various landscapes in life.

Complacency comes in two general forms: conscious complacency and unconscious complacency. Most people do not seek out complacency. It simply slowly overtakes us as we settle into situations in life. This is a hidden danger of spiritual valleys. Once the excitement and newness of an experience with God has worn off, we quickly rest in the reality that we have grown in our relationship with God and celebrate how far we have come. It is easy to move from seeking a period of rest to slipping into an unhealthy complacency.

Complacency is not always easy to recognize in oneself. One good indicator that one is moving toward complacency is the loss of a dynamic understanding of the spiritual journey. Mountains, deserts, and valleys are all dynamic landscapes because they facilitate encounters with God. When we become static in any spiritual landscape, we know that we are approaching complacency. While mountains and deserts, especially oases, have the potential to draw us toward complacency, spiritual valleys, by their very nature, can lull us into an unhealthy attitude of self-satisfaction. There is also conscious complacency: however, few people ever really talk about it. Who among us wants to acknowledge that we, on occasions, consciously reach a stage of complacency, perhaps to avoid a challenge? The Israelites reached this point at Kadesh-barnea (Numbers 13). After a long journey across the desert, they had arrived at the edge of the promised land. Twelve spies were sent out to explore the land. Ten spies returned with a negative report, complaining of large cities and strong people. The people were satisfied to stay in the desert oasis of Kadesh-barnea rather than face the challenges before them. As a result, they were unable to enter the Promised Land and instead wandered in the desert for thirty-eight years. Fear kept them from embracing God and the blessings before them. Complacency was safer. Many of us have faced similar decisions when confronted with the choice either to remain in a place of comfort or adventure into challenges that lie before us on our journey of growth.

Finding resting places, the oases on our sojourn, is vital to a healthy spiritual life. They enable us to reach levels of healthy satisfaction on our spiritual journeys. Valleys provide safe spaces for rest and reflection; however, we must always be mindful not to fall prey to complacency.

Conclusion

It is tempting to look beyond spiritual valleys to mountaintops, where the spiritual highs and feelings of closeness to God reside. Our constant desire to be somewhere else makes it hard to live well in spiritual valleys.

Henri Nouwen reminded us that the spiritual life is not a life beyond our everyday existence. It can only be real when it is lived in the midst of the pains and joys of the here and now.[14] Mindfully living in the present is not always easy. We live in a culture that moves at a very fast pace. Sights and sounds assault us from all directions; strange ideas and demands run through our minds. Multitasking is highly regarded, while contemplation is too often viewed as counter to mainstream culture. This presents certain challenges to embracing the valley as our spiritual home; however, a desire to be more aware of God's presence and to reflect on God's movement in the world opens doors to becoming a valley dweller.

Valley spirituality offers us an exciting way to envision our journey with God. Valleys encourage us to see God in the ordinary and regular things of life. By embracing the incarnational reality, we are empowered to live out a dynamic spiritual life with God and our communities of faith. We come to the realization that our spiritual journey is not restricted to any one landscape, but is in fact a sojourn through various spiritual landscapes of our lives. As we gain a greater awareness of God's presence and become reflective Christians, the Holy Spirit opens our hearts, minds, and imaginations to fresh possibilities of God working in and through us in all of the landscapes of life. Spiritual valleys offer an environment that does not take us to the extreme realms of spiritual possibilities, but instead invites us to become comfortable in the presence of God, embrace the reality that God dwells within us, and learn to see the sacred in the ordinary.

Endnotes

1. Francis de Sales, *Introduction to the Devout Life*, trans. and ed. by John Ryan (New York: Image, 1989), 84.

2. Ibid., 85.

3. Thomas Merton, *New Seeds of Contemplation* (New York: New Direction, 1961), 14.

4. Ronald Rolheiser, *The Holy Longing: The Search for a Christian Spirituality* (New York: Doubleday, 1999), 76.

5. Henri J. M. Nouwen, *Here and Now: Living in the Spirit* (New York: Crossroads, 1997), 135.

6. Rolheiser, *The Holy Longing*, 76.

7. Madeleine L'Engle, *A Circle of Quiet* (New York: HarperCollins, 1972), 49.

8. Esther de Waal, "Attentiveness," *Weavings* 17.4 (2002) 23.

9. Esther de Waal attributes this poem to Merton via a South African monk; "Attentiveness," 22.

10. Belden Lane, *Landscape of the Sacred: Geography and Narrative in American Spirituality* (Baltimore: John Hopkins University Press, 2001), 66.

11. William Dean, *The American Spiritual Culture: And the Invention of Jazz, Football and the Movies* (New York: Continuum, 2002), 57.

12. Nouwen, *Here and Now*, 19.

13. Ibid., 22.

14. Henri J. M. Nouwen, *Making All Things New: An Invitation to the Spiritual Life* (San Francisco: Harper, 1981), 21.

6

Learning to Live in the Presence of God

The sojourn through the pages of this book has opened our imaginations to the reality that we are living in the presence of God through all of the various terrains of life. Mountaintop exhilaration, desert despair, and valley dwelling all awaken us to the unique ways in which God is present in each terrain, inviting us into new dimensions of our faith journey. Slowly, and perhaps even subconsciously, we become more comfortable with God and ourselves as we embrace landscape lessons and begin to dwell mindfully in the presence of God as a natural part of our life.

Landscape lessons, along with the principles of intentionality, desire, and openness, facilitate familiarity and comfort as we journey deeper into the heart of God. Each terrain reveals aspects of our spirituality that allow us to know God and ourselves more fully, stimulating a level of intimacy that has previously been foreign to us. The integrations of principles and lessons allow us to embrace an everyday mysticism with a determination to live out the social implications of our salvation. Our journey also brings us to a point where we understand the need to balance and integrate our individual sojourn into our greater community of faith. Ultimately, our spiritual sojourn is not intended to lead us away from others to isolation on some holy mountain or in a desert cave; on the contrary, our individual growth allows us to share divine grace with others. It allows us to perceive the world through the eyes of God and share divine love as global citizens. Our journey through the various landscapes allows us to see the importance of both an individual spiritual life and its integration into faith communities.

Landscape Lessons

Spiritual mountains, deserts, and valleys invite us to unite the natural rhythm of life with our spiritual journey through sacred terrains. Spiritual mountains stimulate a familiarity with God, giving a deep assurance that God is with us. They are sacred places where we rest in God and experience his blessing. Mountaintops draw on our desire for intimacy with the divine while stimulating trust and faith in God. They often represent the best of what we believe Christianity to be. While mountaintops have numerous weaknesses, which were discussed previously, they exert a powerful draw on our spirits to rejoice and rest with God.

Spiritual deserts provide contrasting experiences to the security and warmth of mountaintops. Deserts have great lessons to teach us. They foster a transparency and vulnerability that comes through struggling with ourselves, our faith, and our God. Spiritual deserts call us to live more authentically, demanding that we let go of our accumulated baggage, embrace God's grace, and recover the kind of spiritual clarity that enables us to see God in places we have never looked. Spiritual deserts furnish us with an unexpected portrait of God and ourselves that is particular to the desert environment. Of all of the spiritual landscapes, perhaps the desert reveals God in the most pure form to our spirits; however, we are often unable or unwilling to see and embrace God in the desert environment. Spiritual valleys simply invite us to embrace the realization that God truly dwells within and among us to enable us to grow in love and grace and become like Christ. Valleys facilitate a greater awareness of God that invites us to view the ordinary as sacred, to see the world, not simply as it appears, but as it can become. Jesus is the highest example of a valley dweller who saw the sacred in the ordinary. He invited us to see and embody God in new and mysterious ways. Jesus revealed a life penetrated by God and expressed divinity on a new level through compassion and love, which still remains as core principles for all faith communities. Valleys give us opportunities for reflection, time and space to listen and commune with God. Collectively, spiritual mountains, valleys, and deserts offer us lessons that prepare us to dwell mindfully in the presence of God, to breathe in the breath of God, to embrace the reality of God's presence in us.

Mindfully Dwelling in the Presence

Ann Wall, Brother Lawrence, and Celtic Christians provide testimonies of those who have combined the lessons from the various landscapes with the principles of intentionality, desire, and openness, all the while learning to dwell mindfully with God. They serve as spiritual guides to assist our journey deeper into God and ourselves. Each of them embodied various lessons and embraced different principles. My friend Ann Wall has spent most of her life in spiritual deserts. She has much to teach us about intentionality and drawing closer to God in the midst of struggles. She is not part of a monastic community or religious order. Ann is simply a Christian on a journey with God through life. Her relationship with God has evolved through a series of crises that have allowed her to reach a level of familiarity, trust, and intimacy with God—a level that some believe is only associated with mountaintop spirituality.

Brother Lawrence, a seventeenth-century French lay brother, provides us with insights into how our desire to be closer to God can turn the mundane routines of life into glorious encounters with God. In a small but influential book, *The Practice of the Presence of God*, Brother Lawrence revealed how to experience the sacred in the ordinary by inviting us to be aware of God in the simplest things of life. He understood that God is always accessible to a seeking heart; and as he went about doing his daily chores, he discovered the beauty of God in the ordinary. He knew that the majority of people would not seek and find God in the midst of the day-to-day experiences of life. Brother Lawrence re-enforced the valley as sacred place by showing the importance of desire in our spiritual sojourn.

Celtic Christians celebrated the entirety of life with a true openness of their minds, hearts, and imaginations toward God. They were sensitive to the presence of God in the natural. They did not easily separate the secular from the sacred, choosing instead to open themselves to God in all things around them. The Celts equally embraced all of life's spiritual landscapes. The imagery of mountains, valleys, and deserts flows throughout their literature.

Celtic Christians lived out a familiarity and intimacy in all of the landscapes. "Thin places" were not limited to spiritual mountains. They extended to the wilderness terrains of Rocky Mountains, harsh deserts, flowering meadows, and storming seas. Ann, Brother Lawrence, and the Celtic Christians all offer us insights that enable a greater awareness and foster comfort as we learn to dwell in the presence of God. These characters combined the principles of intentionality, desire, and openness with the lessons of the spiritual landscapes to direct us toward mindfully dwelling with God.

Lessons From My Friend Ann

Every so often we are blessed to encounter individuals whose lives, although filled with struggles and pain, reflect the qualities of the saints. Those persons' lives are characterized by a deep intentionality to serve God through the various disappointments and celebrations life offers them. My friend Ann is such a person. Her walk with God has been forged by a sojourn through a series of spiritual deserts, which have consumed most of her adult life. She is a desert dweller who has found a spiritual home and intimacy with God in the arid and vast desert terrain.

Early in her life, Ann had a storybook Christian marriage and a beautiful adopted daughter. She and her husband worshiped and served in various ways at a local church. It seemed as if her life was perfect, filled with joy and happiness. But, as with many things in life, circumstances changed, people changed, and relationships changed. Ann's husband began drinking, at first as a social expression with clients, but later in a way that became destructive to himself and others. Other harmful behaviors followed the drinking: unfaithfulness, lies, and abusive treatment toward Ann and the child. Soon the perfect life was only a memory as Ann entered a series of spiritual deserts via crisis. Like so many Christians, Ann valued the mountaintop experiences as reflections of God's blessings and attempted to avoid spiritual deserts as places of punishment. However, due to her circumstances, the desert slowly but surely became a sacred place for Ann, a place where God was very present and real.

It seemed that once her difficulties began, they would never end. A series of circumstances, in addition to those mentioned above, prolonged Ann's desert sojourn. Psychological problems surfaced with her daughter, who continues to struggle with mental and physical disabilities, followed by the loss of her husband to destructive behavior. Ann's own health was not untouched by all the difficulties and issues in her life. In addition to emotional and physical distress from her early years, she struggles with issues related to aging, now in her mid-seventies. She continues to take great responsibility for the care of her middle-aged, semi-disabled daughter; however, a stroke that she suffered a few years ago has slowed her down. A recent fall and the diagnosis of cancer has not affected her perpetual spirit of prayer and determination to bless others. Through all of her struggles, Ann has never lacked intentionality and determination to dwell with God.

Intentionality

Ann's determination and intentionality to walk with God through all of life's landscapes has been foundational for her ministry to others. Her fall and stroke serve only as temporary complications to be overcome through her determination to continue to serve God in whatever ways she can. Ann's intentionality and determination inspire others to realize that spiritual deserts can be sacred places to draw close to God and embrace grace, to look into oneself and release the baggage of life. Much like Jacob wrestling with God, she will not let go, nor will she give up until she is blessed. The Old Testament character Jacob embodied intentionality and determination, although his personality was quite different from that of Ann. Jacob's story is filled with deception. Perhaps the best example of his determination and intentionality is the story of Peniel, the place where he wrestled with God (Genesis 32:22-32). Jacob was about to encounter his brother Esau, from whom he had stolen a birthright. For fear of his brother's anger, he placed his wives and family in a safe place before going on to reflect by himself. During the night, Jacob wrestled with God refusing to let go of the one with whom he struggled. He was determined to hold on at all costs, to struggle with all of his being. He intention was clear: hold on until blessed. Even after his hip was dislocated, he continued his struggle and was blessed, saying, "For I have seen God face to face and yet my life is preserved" (Genesis 32:30).

Difficulties in life serve as opportunities to draw closer to God, to fall into the grace that God offers to all people; however, it requires intentionality and determination. We would prefer to avoid struggles and anything that would cause us pain or suffering, but the reality of life is that pain and suffering are unavoidable. Ann would encourage us to embrace God through the pain and suffering, draw closer, hold on, and rest in the grace one discovers in spiritual deserts.

Release and Embrace

In the midst of her struggles with her husband and daughter, Ann learned to release her burdens to God and rest in the grace that followed. For ten years Ann made the decision to leave her middle-aged daughter in southern California and to travel to Portland, Oregon, to join a college community for a few months each semester. She retired from the public school system in California after thirty-five years of service and decided to spend much of the academic year in Portland working as a volunteer at her alma mater.

Ann's life reflects the transformations that come via the desert. She embodied the lessons of the spiritual desert that had enabled her to dwell with God through the most difficult times of life. She learned to release everything to God and embrace the grace that God offers to all who seek it. Ann's actions were not simply passive acceptance or a willingness to endure suffering. It was faith. Ann chose to see God in places and circumstances that could be easily overshadowed by life's struggle. She, however, intentionally walked with God through the valley of the shadow of death without a clear understanding of outcomes because she discovered grace and a new perspective on life from her desert sojourn. She found a clarity of vision amidst the desert sojourn that inspired her to dwell mindfully with God despite circumstances.

Clarity and Holy Ambiguity

Ann embodied the desert paradox of divine clarity and holy ambiguity. Spiritual deserts eventually bring us to a point of clarity where we are confident of God's presence and direction, yet we often lack specificity. Ann was sure that God continued to call her back to Warner Pacific College each year. Nevertheless, her clarity of purpose and direction was accompanied with ambiguity. How would her daughter function in her absence? Could her daughter drive herself to the doctor's office for regular visits? How would Ann's health hold up during the rainy days in the Pacific Northwest? So many questions were left without clear answers. She relied on what she knew: God had placed her in a wonderful ministry on the college campus. From that knowledge, Ann rested in holy ambiguity, a deep place of faith and trust. She chose to embrace the mystery of God.

Moses, once he agreed to lead the Hebrew children out of Egypt, was clear about the calling; but he did not know exactly how he would accomplish his mission. God did not reveal a detailed plan for delivering a large number of Hebrews. There were no reservations at a desert oasis. No one notified the residents of Palestine that a massive group of people was coming into their land. Moses had clarity of call and a reluctant willingness to embrace holy ambiguity. Holy ambiguity is a point of faith when we trust God based on what we know to be true and rest by faith in divine mystery as we await the details. Such a faith drew Moses closer to God. When Moses entered the tent of meeting, the pillar of cloud, a manifestation of God, descended and Moses spoke to God "face to face, as one speaks to a friend" (Exodus 33:11).

There is much that we can learn from Moses' sojourn with God. Moses maintained a level of intimacy through the physical and metaphorical deserts of his life. He approached God with an authenticity and vulnerability. Moses disagreed, expressed his confusion and disappointments with God, while remaining humble before God as a servant. At no time was Moses afraid of being human in the presence of God, questioning the things he did not understand, but he remained willing to trust God even when he did not understand or agree. Intimacy in a relationship is grounded in openness and honesty. Moses exemplified these characteristics in his relationship with God.

Ann Wall, Moses, Jacob, and countless others provide testimonies of determination and intentionality in their walks with God through the contours of life. They live lives scarred by circumstance; yet they remain witnesses to God's transforming grace, received and embodied in the deepest levels of their being through struggle. They live the words of Brother Lawrence, "we need to be faithful even in dry periods. We should take advantage of those times to practice our determination and our surrender to Him [God]. This will often bring us to a maturity further on in our walk with God."[1] In Ann's case, as in the case of Moses, spiritual deserts have drawn her closer to God. She has become a desert dweller who draws strength from her experiences. Ann utilizes her sojourn to minister to others who struggle to understand God during periods of suffering. She can teach us how to live mindfully in the presence of God through the difficult landscapes of life.

Lessons From Brother Lawrence

The Practice of the Presence of God is an enduring spiritual classic by a little known lay brother named Lawrence of the Resurrection. Most of the information we have about Lawrence (Nicholas Herman) comes through his friend Joseph de Beaufort, who wrote an account of the *Life of Brother Lawrence* shortly after the monk's death in 1691. *The Practice of the Presence of God* is a collection of conversations, letters, and spiritual maxims that has influenced sinners and saints for centuries. Reflecting Lawrence's close connection to daily life, the book draws its power from its simplicity and practicality.

Brother Lawrence suggested that we can remain aware of God's presence throughout each day, regardless of what we are doing, simply by talking with God. It would be an error to think that one would need to abandon conversations with God in order to deal with the world.[2] His practical advice to lay brothers and monks helped them to be aware of the sacred in the ordinary. Brother Lawrence's works offer us a gift: to see God in the ordinary, to reflect on the simplest things of life as encounters with God, and to increase our general spiritual awareness. These are all outgrowths of a deep desire to serve God and grow in grace.

Desire

Desire was foundational for Brother Lawrence. He longed for God above all else. Desire is essential for any form of spirituality—not just any desire, but a deep spiritual desire to dwell with God. Neither skill nor knowledge is needed to sit with God. All that is necessary is a heart dedicated entirely to God, a heart filled with desire for God.[3] King David, whose life reflected a wide range of human experiences and struggles, was said to be a man after God's own heart (1 Samuel 13:14). King David had a deep desire to serve God, even though he had many faults and failures. His desire motivated his relationship with God through times of celebrations and times of sin. God looks at the desire of our hearts and the motivation of our spirits to determine our intentions. Our desires can be selfish and our motives are sometimes shrouded by our attempts to justify our desires. We are flawed human beings struggling towards perfection; however, Brother Lawrence and King David did not allow their flaws to get in the way of their desire to walk with God.

When my daughter was born, I realized an entirely new dimension of desire. Lindsey was our first child. I thought the world stopped the day she was born, at least long enough to appreciate the miracle that she was. I hated to travel and to be away from her for any length of time. My heart was overjoyed just to hold and play with her. Time just seemed to cease when I was with Lindsey. My family still makes fun of the hours of videotapes I took of her just lying in her baby bed. For the first time in my life, I realized what true desire was. It had nothing to do with *wanting* pizza and a diet coke or *dreaming* of owning a home someday. No longer could I refer to those types of things as desires. I now understand desire to be a deep longing that grows from one's heart and penetrates the entirety of one's being. I began to understand what it means to desire to walk closely with God, not in a superficial matter, but from a deep longing to be with, to sit with, and to talk with God. This is the type of desire Brother Lawrence advocated. This type of desire leads us to a greater awareness of God in all of life and is foundational for those who want to dwell mindfully with God.

Awareness

Awareness is central to Brother Lawrence's teachings about practicing the presence of God. "The presence of God is the concentration of the soul's attention on God, remembering that God is always present."[4] This is the type of spiritual awareness that enables us to dwell mindfully with God. Brother Lawrence's writings invite us to discover God in the simplest places, in the ordinary things of life. He beckons us to see the world as a beautiful place in which the ordinary reveals the sacred. God is always accessible simply through our desire to practice the divine presence.

Lawrence believed that all spiritual life consisted of practicing God's presence and that anyone who practiced it correctly would soon attain spiritual fulfillment.[5] The desire to sit humbly with God and allow the conversation to progress without limitations is required for those who truly seek to dwell with God. This communication does not require anything more than an open heart and a willingness to listen patiently. According to Brother Lawrence, "The most holy and necessary practice in our spiritual life is the presence of God. That means finding constant pleasure in His divine company, speaking humbly and lovingly with Him in all seasons, at every moment, without limiting the conversation in any way. This is especially important in times of temptation, sorrow, separation from God, and even in times of unfaithfulness and sin."[6] The simplest way for Brother Lawrence to communicate with God was to simply do his ordinary work. Washing dishes, sweeping floors, preparing a meal—all things served as opportunities to commune with God. Churches and chapels were not required in order to dwell in God's presence. A desire to commune with God transformed every place into a sacred place. "It isn't necessary that we stay in church in order to remain in God's presence. We can make our heart a chapel where we can go anytime to talk to God privately."[7] Some places naturally inspire our awareness of God; however, if we open ourselves to the reality that God is dwelling within us, then any place and every place, whether mountain, desert, or valley, is a sacred place to commune with God.

Mindfully Dwelling with God

Some three hundred years after his death, Brother Lawrence continues to aid us in our quest to dwell mindfully with God. The results of a life given to practicing the presence of God can be summed up in four points. First, faith is livelier and more active in our lives."[8] This is particularly evident when we travel through spiritual deserts. Brother Lawrence suggested that a soul accustomed to practicing God's presence is able to navigate through difficulty with greater ease. When we naturally enter into God's presence as a regular spiritual exercise, life's struggles only serve to move us to a familiar place, into the arms of God. Second, practice of the presence of God strengthens us in hope. Our hope increases as our faith penetrates God's heart. As we discover the beauty of God, we begin to see the ordinary as sacred and the normal as holy. Third, we experience an overwhelming joy from the knowledge that we are always with God. We reach a point where God's presence seems natural to us. We are set "aglow with the fire of holy love. The soul thus inflamed can no longer live except in the presence of God."[9] Lawrence spoke of a point in our spiritual relationship when we are driven by a holy urgency to dwell with God. Finally, practicing the presence of God leads us to grow in "continual acts of love, praise, confidence, thanksgiving, offering, and petition." [10]

In short, Brother Lawrence shapes our desire for God into a practice of mindful presence. This "practice of the presence of God" invites us to see the sacred in the ordinary and the holy in the mundane. For a life centered in God, everything can be an expression of God or an act of worship, from washing dishes in the kitchen to driving children on a school bus. Brother Lawrence bids us to focus our desire, open our minds to God's movement, and mindfully dwell in the presence of the holy.

Lessons from the Celtic Spiritual Tradition

Any conversation connecting landscape spirituality and living in the presence of God would be incomplete without some reference to Celtic Christianity. The Celts were mindful of the "thin places" in life, those mountaintop moments that permeated all of life's landscapes. Celtic Christians embraced a deep sense of God's presence in the here and now, understanding the Divine as immediate and accessible.[11] Their passionate pursuit of God in all of life, sensitized them to divine expressions in the ordinary—in life, love, eating, working, and playing.[12] All of life was an opportunity for God's expressions. Nature, landscapes, animals, and fellow humans were all means to experience God's grace. The Celts held a mystical and imaginative understanding of life that allowed them to embrace all of creation as an expression of God's immanence. Thus, God was understood as one who walked alongside, a companion on the journey of adventure and discovery. Celtic Christians opened themselves to the movements of God, seeking thin places where the veil between the divine and human grew transparent. This type of openness is a gift to those who journey through various spiritual terrains.

Openness

An openness to God's presence in all of creation facilitated the Celts' ability to dwell mindfully in the presence of God. In a way, they recaptured the essence of Eden by opening themselves to God's movements around them. They were not quick to separate the secular from the sacred, to define that which is understood as holy against those things that were not. Their world-view necessitated an openness to God in everything. "God was present to them in images and signs, poetry and art, in sacrament and liturgy."[13] The Welsh poem "Glorious Lord" is an example of the rich openness Celts demonstrated toward God.

> Hail to you, glorious Lord!
> May church and chancel praise you,
> May plain and hillside praise you,
> May the three springs praise you,
> Two higher than the wind and one above the earth,
> May darkness and light praise you,
> The cedar and the sweet fruit tree.
> Abraham praised you, the founder of faith,
> May life everlasting praise you,
> May the birds and the bees praise you,
> Aaron and Moses praised you,

May male and female praise you,
May the seven days and the stars praise you,
May the lower and upper air praise you,
May books and letters praise you,
May the fish in the river praise you,
May thought and action praise you,
May the sand and the earth praise you,
May all the good things created praise you,
And I too shall praise you, Lord of glory,
Hail to you, glorious Lord![14]

The poem reads like a psalter of praise, an account of creation's accolades to God. The entire world serves as an instrument of praise to God, and we too are invited to add our voices to the great choirs.

Our world stimulates guarded trust and suspicion. Many have difficulty opening themselves up to both God and others because it requires risk, vulnerability, and trust. These are characteristics that our society does not often encourage. We are afraid of being hurt, violated, or deceived. Openness requires risk, along with willingness to engage honestly with one another with authenticity and love. Openness leads to a greater awareness, which in turn brings us to a place of trust and authentic relationships.

Our culture, however, continues to encourage and popularize messages of deceit that undermine the value of openness. Network reality television programs like "Joe Millionaire One and Two," "The Cheat," "The Mole," and, on a different, yet still powerful level, "Survivor" and "Bachelor and Bachelorette," depend on deception and stand contrary to openness and trust. At the center of each of these programs lies an artificial trust and openness, but success ultimately depends on deception. It is not surprising that most of the relationships developed through these programs do not last. In addition, it is not surprising that many Americans struggle with trust, relationships, authentic community, and an openness to God and one another.

Society is filled with messages that undermine openness and trust. We live in environments that stimulate guardedness and desensitize us. Celtic Christianity can aid us in reclaiming an openness to God and expressions of divine grace and love in the world. All of life's landscapes—

mountains, deserts, and valleys—invite an awareness and openness to the divine. While we cannot simply recapture the Celtic world, we can embrace their insights to aid us in our journey with God in the twenty-first century.

Thin Places

The Celts' openness to the divine stimulated their relationship with God. They were not so quick to separate the visible and invisible, or the material and spiritual. Instead, they perceived the world being woven together as one beautiful expression of God's presence. The Celts were sensitive to life's "thin places" and willing to embrace them. Thin places are those places and moments when the invisible and spiritual are more accessible to us. These are the moments when our perceived separation from God is lessened, when the walls we have built around ourselves are broken down and the distance between us and God becomes thin and transparent.

Thin and sacred spaces are places "where we stand still in awe, where the barrier between our time-bound and our eternity-seeking selves is lowered."[15] Thin places serve as sacraments; "they encapsulate something of the mystery towards which they point, and help to make this mystery real and incarnated in our human lives."[16] Marcus Borg suggests that "a thin place is a sacrament of the sacred, a mediator of the sacred, a means whereby the sacred becomes present to us. A thin place is a means of grace."[17] These thin and sacred places stimulate the imagination, allowing the invisible to connect the consciousness of our heart and mind. These places mark points of divine penetration into the world and invite us to glimpse the transcendent. Thin places often become sites to establish churches or monasteries or, more simply, to erect stone monuments and high crosses. They invite us not only to remember the divine encounter marked by a symbol, but also to encounter God within the place itself.

Openness and awareness of God's movement in the world are the key elements to discovering thin places. We all have experienced thin places, those instances when time stops and we are caught in the moment. A first kiss, the birth of a first-born, the fall of the sun on the horizon—these are examples of thin places. Sometimes thin places are almost unperceivable to us while at other times they overwhelm us. Thin places tend to suspend us in a moment when time stops and God reaches into us.

Mountaintop experiences often serve as thin places, which is why we long to linger at the summit and soak in the beauty of the vista. During these experiences the distance between us and the divine is greatly lessened and we see, feel, hear, and touch God in ways that are all too unfamiliar to us. However, we should not limit our understandings of thin places to mountaintop moments. Desert and valley landscapes invite us into places of struggle and reflection where the divine breaks into the human. In the Celtic tradition, thin places were often wilderness landscapes in harsh coastal environments like Skellig Michael, "a desert in the ocean".[18] If the noise of the world threatens to drown out the call of God, we need to create silence and space, our own desert in the ocean.[19]

Thin places can emerge from almost anywhere. A thin place can be at a piano, as one ad-libs various styles of music, or beside a child's bed during conversations about the world before bedtime prayers. Moments surrounding birth and death are often thin places where the invisible breaks in on the visible. Thin places are "personal to each of us, but they are the space in which we are drawn to an inclusive wholeness where we are all one in unity. They are places of community, sacred for each, sacred to all."[20] These sacred and thin places draw us to divine familiarity and community.

The Celts learned how to dwell in the presence of God by maintaining connections between the secular and the sacred, the material and the spiritual, the visible and the invisible. They lived out the incarnational reality of God's indwelling presence. The Celts spoke of God dwelling in the world and in their lives in such a way that Emmanuel, God with us, became a reality.[21] Incarnational reality requires the same from us. If we seek to dwell mindfully in God's presence, we must embrace the reality that God is living in, through, and with us already. This type of familiarity does not come through casual contact, but through intentionality and commitment to discovery and exploration.

Conclusion

Ann, Brother Lawrence, and Celtic Christians discovered how to dwell mindfully with God through the various experiences of life. They knew that God offers grace and love to us throughout our journey, regardless of the circumstances or terrain. They learned to be aware of, and rest in, God's presence as they sensed the movement of the divine, each in their own way.

If we receive the blessings that each landscape offers to us, we will see the world in a new way and live out our spirituality with a vitality that has too long been absent. We need not join isolated religious communities or retreat away from the world to dwell mindfully with God. We simply need to open ourselves to the reality that God is present in every terrain of life and change our expectations of extra-ordinary spirituality to allow for the revelation of the sacred in the ordinary. If we can embrace God in all of the spiritual landscapes of life, we will begin to live within the divine familiarity offered to us so freely. Intentionality, desire, and openness, combined with the lessons of each landscape, empower a spirituality rooted in God, lived out in individuals, and expressed in community.

Endnotes

1. Brother Lawrence, *The Practice of the Presence of God* (Springdale, Pa.: Whitaker, 1982), 9.
1. Ibid., 8.
2. Ibid., 17.
3. Ibid., 67.
4. Ibid., 29.
5. Ibid., 59.
6. Ibid., 33.
7. Ibid., 71.
8. Ibid., 72.
9. Ibid.
10. Esther de Waal, *The Celtic Way of Prayer: The Recovery of the Religious Imagination* (New York: Doubleday, 1997), 69.
11. Timothy Joyce, *Celtic Christianity: A Sacred Tradition, A Vision of Hope* (Maryknoll, N.Y.: Orbis, 1998), 154.
12. Oliver Davis, *Celtic Spirituality,* Classics of Western Spirituality (New York: Paulist, 1999), 3.
13. Poem quoted as printed in Davis, *Celtic Spirituality,* 267.
14. Margaret Silf, *Sacred Spaces: Stations on a Celtic Way* (Brewster, Mass.: Paraclete, 2001), 9.
15. Ibid.
16. Marcus Borg, *The Heart of Christianity: Rediscovering a Life of Faith* (San Francisco: HarperSanFrancisco, 2003), 156.

17. David Adam entitled one of his books *A Desert in the Ocean: The Spiritual Journeys According to St. Brendan the Navigator* (New York: Paulist, 2000). It is a phrase he took from Adamnan's *Life of Columba*.
18. Ibid., 14.
19. Silf, *Sacred Spaces*, 9.
20. Esther de Waal, *The Celtic Way of Prayer*, 70.

Conclusion

Spirituality in general, and Christian spirituality specifically, is a moving target that refuses to be contained in any box. Using landscape metaphors to articulate the spiritual journey is not an attempt to create a new container to confine and control the Christian spiritual journey. Landscape metaphors attempt to free pilgrims from limited paradigms and worn out images that have not stimulated the spiritual imagination, facilitated a greater awareness of God, nor encouraged spiritual reflection. These metaphors guide the imagination into sacred spaces where our understandings of God and ourselves can be expanded. Landscape metaphors allow us to explore spirituality through the use of imagery that taps into common experiences and language that encourages spiritual reflection, allowing us to discover deeper dimensions of our faith.

I want to return to two key points that are central to the type of spiritual growth encouraged in this book: the recovery of the art of spiritual reflection and the renewing and recreating of authentic communities of faith. Raising spiritual expectations and providing guidance to navigate life's spiritual landscapes will accomplish little if communities of faith are unable to facilitate the growing needs for genuine community and instruct pilgrims in the art of spiritual reflection.

Spiritual reflection does not flow naturally from our hearts and minds; however, our journey through life's landscapes stimulates the spiritually reflective process. The experiences from our sojourn through various terrains bring us to the doorstep of reflection and demand recognition. Spiritual reflection requires us to open ourselves to the movement of God's Spirit. As we sit with experiences and thoughts, we allow God to speak into our hearts and minds through ordinary and extra-ordinary events of our lives. It is only through spiritual reflection that we will start to remember what God looks like, sounds like, moves like, and feels like. Our ability to be spiritually reflective flows more naturally as our awareness grows and develops.

Unlike mountaintop encounters, the desert sojourn becomes sacred for us only after a period of spiritual reflection. Most pilgrims are unable to see the desert as sacred place because intense emotions overwhelm them and impede their abilities to sit with God and reflect on the baggage they struggle to leave behind. Spiritual deserts demand that we reflect on the environment through which we travel before we can begin to understand that God's presence has never been any further away than the air that we breathe. The struggles of our desert sojourn simply serve to reveal our hearts and hurts, our fears and follies, our need for healing and hope. The desert oasis provides a much needed rest as well as an opportunity to reflect on the desert journey and its lessons.

Spiritual reflection is perhaps hardest to conjure up in the valley. Valleys often conceal the holy in the ordinary, leaving us unaware of the divine experiences unfolding all around us. Holy moments go unnoticed by the unreflective heart and mind, and sacred encounters are lost. Valleys are the common places of our lives, waiting to be transformed into the sacred through spiritual reflection.

While spiritual reflection is central for our individual sojourn, it finds support, direction, and, to a degree, definition from our faith communities. However, we live in a period when spirituality has reached beyond the confines of organized religious communities into mainstream culture and media. Many Christians have found support, direction, and some definition for their spiritual journey in and through popular culture. In the past, the church and the Bible served as foundations from which spirituality was constructed and understood; however, for a growing segment of Christians, God is expressed and experienced in various forms: other people, art, literature, music, nature, movies, television, architecture, the Bible, and on occasions, even the church. In short, American culture is a *locus theologicus*, a "theological place," and has a growing influence and impact on Christian spirituality.[1]

Popular culture serves as a major source for the forming and informing of Christian spirituality. The reshaping of our concepts and expectations of community is one example of pop culture's influence. The popular television series "Friends" stands as a formative example of community. A group of friends, with all the regular problems of life, share a commitment to each other to journey together through life's various terrains. Their community fosters authenticity, demands mutual responsibility, and generates an unconditional love that embraces imperfections while bringing out the best in one another. This electronic community has formed and shaped our understanding and expectations for what authentic community means. Genuine community strikes at the heart of what so many people are searching for. This is why community continues to be a major theme of television programming.

Sitcoms are not the only place that our understanding and experience of community is being shaped. Oprah, the spiritual sage of daytime television, functions pastorally to millions of viewers all over the world as she daily addresses relevant topics of life. She forms an electronic community of authenticity that, in its own way, facilitates an eclectic spirituality of self-awareness, angelic powers, and spiritual guides. She expresses compassion and concern, while optimizing her position, influence, and finances, to transform the lives of her viewers. Oprah has become a spiritual mother to America and the world, as was shown by her leadership of the memorial service for the victims of the 9/11 attacks held in Yankee Stadium shortly after the attacks. She led the nation and the world through a service of sorrow and hope. Oprah's spirituality, like that of many Americans, is based in Christianity; but it incorporates various other practices and ideologies. That is one reason why so many people relate to her.

In addition to sitcoms and Oprah, cyber spiritual communities attract pilgrims as they search for fulfillment and direction. Cyber spiritual communities continue to grow and evolve in the form of virtual sanctuaries, online labyrinths, and interactive web sites that explore scripture in creative ways. Christians are seeking communities to live out their faith experiences. The church no longer functions as the sole provider of spiritual direction and community for Christians.

Ecclesiastical communities must overcome their reputations for infighting and narrow-minded ideologies that work against authentic community if they hope to be relevant in the twenty-first century. Churches are too often "be like us" organizations that require conformity more than authenticity. Although inclusive congregational labels portray openness to others, the openness is often limited to those who share a common ideology. Those who do not, soon find themselves rejected. Meanwhile, other congregations do not even attempt to be inclusive, but clearly state, through a variety of means, who is welcome and who is not. People want to belong to a community that embraces imperfections, requires mutual accountability, fosters authenticity, and expresses unconditional love. These are characteristics of authentic community, characteristics that cannot be falsified.

Authentic spiritual communities cannot be constructed from the lectures or presentations of seminar speakers. It is not something that can be faked for the purpose of church growth. Dietrich Bonhoeffer reminded us that genuine community is not an ideal, but a divine reality. It is a spiritual not a psychic reality.[2] Authentic community flows from the hearts and minds of people who honestly seek to draw closer to God and who are willing to join together with others in their imperfections as pilgrims on a journey. Authentic community provides safe spaces for people to raise hard questions of faith; it offers support during the spiritual struggles that ensue; it stimulates spiritual exploration, while inspiring discovery. Authentic community is a gift from God, rooted in Jesus, beyond the creation of humanity.

The spiritual journey is a timeless part of the human experience. How we articulate and enable the journey is left to the poets, artists, musicians, writers, storytellers, and theologians of our time—people who inspire our imaginations. These spiritual agitators stimulate our search for meaning, purpose, identity, and belonging. Through a variety of means, these prophetic characters consciously and unconsciously call us to engage in the spiritual journey, while raising hard questions of the faith. Mountain, desert, and valley landscapes are simply avenues to begin the conversations concerning divine awareness, spiritual reflection, and authentic community. These metaphorical landscapes strike a common chord that enables us to sit together, experience authentic community, and share our journeys with one another while we grow deeper and closer to God and each other.

Endnotes

1. Andrew Greeley, *God in Popular Culture* (Chicago: Thomas More, 1988), 9.
2. Dietrich Bonhoeffer, *Life Together,* trans. John W. Doberstein (New York: Harper, 1954), 26. Bonhoeffer contrasts spiritual and psychic as the apostle Paul did spirit and flesh. His intent is to distinguish God's graceful action from human, self-centered action. In short, genuine community is a gift from God to those who come together in Christ. It cannot be created through human action apart from God.

Bibliography

Adam, David. *A Desert in the Ocean: The Spiritual Journeys according to St. Brendan the Navigator*. New York: Paulist, 2000.

Bonhoeffer, Dietrich. *Life Together*. Translated by John W. Doberstein. New York: Harper, 1954.

Borg, Marcus. *The Heart of Christianity: Rediscovering a Life of Faith*. San Francisco: HarperSanFrancisco, 2003.

Brueggemann, Walter. *The Spirituality of the Psalms*. Facets. Minneapolis: Fortress Press, 2002.

Davis, Oliver. *Celtic Spirituality*. Classics of Western Spirituality. New York: Paulist, 1999.

Dean, William. *The American Spiritual Culture: And the Invention of Jazz, Football and the Movies*. New York: Continuum, 2002.

de Waal, Esther. "Attentiveness." *Weavings* 27.4 (2002).

———. *The Celtic Way of Prayer: The Recovery of the Religious Imagination*. New York: Doubleday, 1997.

Greeley, Andrew. *The Catholic Imagination*. Berkeley: Univ. of California Press, 2000.

————. *God in Popular Culture.* Chicago: Thomas More, 1988.

Gregory of Nyssa. *The Life of Moses.* Translated by Abraham J. Malherbe and Everett Ferguson. Cistercian Studies 31. New York: Paulist, 1978.

Johnson, Spencer. *The Precious Present.* New York: Doubleday, 1984.

Joyce, Timothy. *Celtic Christianity: A Sacred Tradition, A Vision of Hope.* Maryknoll, N.Y.: Orbis, 1998.

Kearney, Richard. *Poetics of Imagining: Modern to Post-Modern.* Perspectives in Continental Philosophy 6. New York: Fordham Univ. Press, 1998.

Keating, Thomas. *Crisis of Faith, Crisis of Love.* New York: Continuum, 2000.

————. *Invitation to Love: The Way of Christian Contemplation.* New York: Continuum, 1994.

Lane, Belden. *Landscape of the Sacred: Geography and Narrative in American Spirituality.* Baltimore: Johns Hopkins University Press, 2001.

————. *The Solace of Fierce Landscapes: Exploring Desert and Mountain Spirituality.* New York: Oxford Univ. Press, 1998.

Lawrence of the Resurrection, Brother. *The Practice of the Presence of God.* Springdale, Pa.: Whitaker, 1982.

L'Engle, Madeleine. *A Circle of Quiet.* San Francisco: HarperCollins, 1972.

McFague, Sallie. *Speaking in Parables: A Study in Metaphor and Theology.* Philadelphia: Fortress, 1975.

McLaren, Brian. *A New Kind of Christian: A Tale of Two Friends on a Spiritual Journey.* San Francisco: Jossey-Bass, 2001.

Merton, Thomas. *Contemplation in a World of Action.* Notre Dame: Univ. of Notre Dame Press, 1998.

————. *New Seeds of Contemplation.* New York: New Direction, 1961.

Nouwen, Henri J. M. *Here and Now: Living in the Spirit.* New York: Crossroads, 1997.

———. *Intimacy.* San Francisco: Harper, 1969.

———. *Making All Things New: An Invitation to the Spiritual Life.* San Francisco: Harper, 1981.

———. *The Path of Peace.* New York: Crossroad, 1995.

Ochs, Carol, and Kerry Olitzky. *Jewish Spiritual Guidance: Finding Our Way to God.* San Francisco: Jossey-Bass, 1997.

Palmer, Parker. *Let Your Life Speak: Listening for the Voice of Vocation.* San Francisco: Jossey-Bass, 2000.

Parks, Sharon Daloz. *Big Questions, Worthy Dreams: Mentoring Young Adults in Their Search for Meaning, Purpose, and Faith.* San Francisco: Jossey-Bass, 2000.

Rolheiser, Ronald. *The Holy Longing: The Search for a Christian Spirituality.* New York: Doubleday, 1999.

Sales, Francis de. *Introduction to the Devout Life,* trans. and ed. by John Ryan. New York: Image, 1989.

Seaward, Brian Luke. *Stand Like Mountain, Flow Like Water: Reflections on Stress and Human Spirituality.* Deerfield Beach, Fla.: Health Communications, 1997.

Silf, Margaret. *Sacred Spaces: Stations on a Celtic Way.* Brewster, Mass.: Paraclete, 2001.

Swan, Laura. *The Forgotten Desert Mothers: Sayings, Lives and Stories of Early Christian Women.* New York: Paulist, 2001.

Wright, Wendy M. "Desert Listening." *Weavings* 9.3 (1994) 6–16.